36

Dr Swati Lodha is an author, 'lifelong kindergartener' and dedicated daughter–wife–mom. Currently, she is the director of MET Institute of Management, Mumbai.

She is the author of *Beyond the Blue* (2021), *Who Is Revathi Roy?* (2019), *54 Reasons Why Parents Suck and Phew!* (2018), *Don't Raise Your Children, Raise Yourself* (2016) and other bestselling books like *Why Women are What They Are* (2004) and *Come On! Get Set Go* (2002).

With a PhD in women entrepreneurship, she is passionate about creativity and innovation. Apart from being an author, social entrepreneur and corporate trainer, she has been director of many B-schools across the country.

She founded her first venture Swash Personality Development Private Limited 24 years ago which offers training courses to youths, professionals and women.

She has mentored more than 12,000 individuals from different walks of life. She is a mentor to many upcoming entrepreneurs and writes for many digital platforms on leadership, motivation and personal excellence.

Connect with her on:
Website: www.drswatilodha.com
Facebook: https://www.facebook.com/Dr.SwatiLodha/
Twitter: @Dr_Swati_Lodha
LinkedIn: https://www.linkedin.com/in/drswatilodha

360 Degree

EXCEL AT ANYTHING AND EVERYTHING

Swati Lodha

RUPA

First published by
Rupa Publications India Pvt. Ltd 2022
7/16, Ansari Road, Daryaganj
New Delhi 110002

Copyright © Swati Lodha 2022
Illustrations by Swaraa Lodha

The views and opinions expressed in this book are the author's own and the
facts are as reported by her which have been verified to the extent possible,
and the publishers are not in any way liable for the same.

P-ISBN: 978-93-9054-715-9
E-ISBN: 978-93-9054-724-1

Second impression 2024

10 9 8 7 6 5 4 3 2

The moral right of the author has been asserted.

To the infinite potential in each one of us

CONTENTS

Preface   *ix*

Introduction   *xiii*

1. Excellence 360 Degree   1

2. Self-Teaming   28

3. And Gaming   47

4. P Pedestalling   77

5. Transfer Learning   103

6. Perennialling   146

Epilogue   174

Acknowledgements   176

PREFACE

Each book brews inside the writer for a long time before they finally decide to commit to it. This book, too, has lived inside me for the longest time. I would have liked to write it at the earliest because as a reader, it would have helped me pivot at several profound junctures of my life and saved me many a painful experience as a professional, a partner and as a parent. However, unfortunately, I could not write it earlier—not before going through all that I experienced in the last two decades of my life in the different roles that I chose.

In 1997, I became a parent to my start-up, Swash (though I wasn't aware of the term 'start-up' then). Swash offered life skill programmes for children, adolescents and professionals, certified by a foreign university (Harding University, USA). I had to persist to make it work. For a 21-year-old girl, hurdles and hiccups begin at home. I was already married when I was pursuing the last leg of my MBA (Master of Business Administration) programme. Though I married for love, it does not essentially make someone believe in you. I believed in my partner for life, but somehow, he found it difficult to believe in my idea of training young minds to be confident, decisive and effective speakers.

At my workshops, I often say, in jest, that my marriage was a start-up, as it was fraught with real risk. After all, I did not have the luxury of putting the blame on my family if something went wrong. To everyone's astonishment, both the start-ups worked, enriching me with memories—mundane and miraculous, terrible and terrific, awful and awesome.

Swash was a movement through which I dreamt of shaping young minds into confident, courageous and authentic individuals. After a few weeks of making a difference in the lives of teenagers and adolescents through my courses, my husband, Shailesh Lodha could finally see the potential, and together, we marched till he relocated to pursue his other dream—that of pursuing acting. Swash gave me valuable insights as a professional, a parent and as a person. I learnt to build a business with conscience, a finishing school for the mind where our personal involvement and authentic responses mattered the most.

I saw parents and children of all ages, having fears and fantasies of their own. Some felt horrible and helpless. Some were scared and faceless. I came face to face with stereotypes ruining lives. I witnessed blatant gender biases and social stigmatization.

In the meantime, my daughter, Swaraa was born. I became a real parent. As a founder of Swash, teenagers and adolescents merely spent some part of their lives with me. They felt a difference and then moved on. Now that I had the 'real deal', I came to understand why parenting is like getting a tattoo on the face—you need to be 100 per cent convinced and there's no turning back. I was already a writer by then, with two published poetry collections. However, after the birth of my daughter, she was the only poetry I wrote in the next 18 years. All I wrote was prose: books, theses and coursework.

From 2002 to 2009, I worked as a director of a now-defunct B-school (Jodhpur Institute of Management) while raising my start-up Swash and my daughter Swaraa. Being a solitary woman at that position, among many senior male directors, several questions arose in my mind. Why was it that my male colleagues interrupted me in meetings? How difficult was it for them to acknowledge my presence on the table? As I met and conversed with other senior female professionals, I had more questions in my mind regarding my role as a mother and a manager, that of being a founder and a nurturer.

I had to change cities to be with my husband. Therefore, I left Swash behind and resurrected my personal and professional life in Mumbai, first as the director of a B-school and then as a solopreneur. I matured as a partner as I navigated through gender bias and patriarchy, while noticing nuances of patronizing attitudes as social conditioning. I was fortunately born in a gender-agnostic family, where my parents never fussed about not having a boy, expecting both their daughters to excel professionally. No one expects a person to prepare to be a wife and a mother. These roles are believed to come naturally. After marriage, another form of patriarchy manifested, where women had their meals only after the male members had eaten and the men asserted they be respected as heads of the family.

With my daughter growing up, questions multiplied and crossed floors. The questions they had for me as a mother, the leader in me was able to better understand and answer. What the leader in me questioned, the parent in me had a solution to.

Now, I am an empty nester and an intermittent caregiver to my two sets of parents—my own and my in-laws. Each passing day, there are group phone calls made to different parts of the world to connect with my daughter and all parents. There are mixed feelings about balancing their autonomy and safety. We are anxious to keep them safe, while they are eager to stay independent. In the middle of feeling sandwiched, I feel the need to plan for my platinum years— to have a more rewarding second career and purposeful use of time.

All these experiences as a person, partner, professional and parent in the last two decades prompted me to write this book about excelling in not one, not two but all of these roles. We should do it because we can. We did not give it a try because no one ever expected us to do so well. Not only 5G phones, 5D lives are possible too; the five dimensions of being a person, a partner, a parent, a professional and a perennial. Read the book and give it a shot.

INTRODUCTION

A master in the art of living draws no sharp distinction between his work and his play; his labour and his leisure, his mind and his body, his education and his recreation. He hardly knows which is which. He simply pursues his vision of excellence through whatever he is doing, and leaves others to determine whether he is working or playing. To himself, he always appears to be doing both.

—Lawrence Pearsall Jacks

It was a humid July evening. My flight to Ahmedabad was delayed. By the time I entered the campus of the Indian Institute of Management (IIM) Ahmedabad, one of the country's premier B-schools, it was around 9 p.m. It was quiet and serene. Even the faint sound of the opening of the car door seemed to disturb the quietness. At the reception of the building where I was supposed to check in for the following week, I met another female guest (Nidhi Arora). We exchanged a smile and started chatting. After checking in, we went straight to the mess to grab a bite. After spending an hour together, we felt like we were destined to meet each other.

In the next one week of my stay there, I learnt from Nidhi that power dynamics between a man and a woman, between an influencer and the influenced, can be balanced and life can be more dignified and joyful for both.

Her theories on life got me thinking and I started noting them down. Since I was working on a parenting book at that time, I got busy with it. The next year, in 2014, I attended an executive education programme at Harvard Kennedy School, where we were expected to present an adaptive leadership[1] challenge. I asked the 65 participants attending the programme, who were mostly senior professionals, from 19 countries, if parenting could teach leaders a few things and vice versa. Seventy-five per cent of them agreed that parenting had made them far more effective as leaders and that leadership skills indeed helped them hone their parenting skills. In fact, Stewart D. Friedman and Alyssa F. Westring had, at the time, endorsed the concept of adaptive leadership in their book *Parents Who Lead*.[2]

In 2014, what started as a quest for connecting parenting and leadership eventually turned into an expansive exploration of excelling multidimensionally—as a person, a professional, a partner and a parent. I am grateful to extraordinary people like Dr Tererai Trent, Ray Dalio, Justice Leila Seth, Satya Nadella, Briana Williams,

---

[1]Adaptive leadership is a practical approach to solving business issues, guiding leaders in identifying and focusing on the important aspects of a business operation and discarding what it can do without.

[2]Friedman, Stewart D. and Alyssa F. Westring, *Parents Who Lead: The Leadership Approach You Need to Parent with Purpose, Fuel Your Career, and Create a Richer Life*, Harvard Business Review Press, 2020.

Onler Kom, Rahul Dravid and my friend Nidhi Arora, on whose footprints I treaded to test my five principles (discussed during the course of the book).

This book sums up my collective quest, the exploration and outcomes of the last two decades of playing different roles and learning from many in person and through findings frozen in research journals and books about being your best version, in every walk of life.

You will find more anecdotes, supporting theories and actionable plans on my blog FindyourSpice (findyourspice. in). Together, we can create a great pool of sharable knowledge if you share your experiences with 'Holistic Heroism' and how it is going while you make changes in your life to embrace 'Excellence 360 degree'.

It is not only the beginning of this book, but also the beginning of a movement.

EXCELLENCE 360 DEGREE

THE SPYCE WOMAN

Clad in a silk saree, with the smallest possible bindi adorning her forehead, there is much about this woman that stands out as unusual.

On the surface, she is one of those IIM grads meant to have an envy-evoking career. But as I scratch the surface, I meet a unique person, a promising professional, a path-breaking partner and a passionate parent. She is a poetess and a problem-solver. She is a team player and a team leader. As a senior professional, she has excelled in project management, strategy, HR, IT and CSR, but she is an entrepreneur too. As a partner, her ways are path-breaking as she has a special financial agreement with her life partner. She is a passionate parent to her son Ishaan and her lean, non-profit organization, Esha.

She is Nidhi Arora, an ordinary woman with an extraordinary will to excel—as a professional, a partner, a parent as well as a person. Born in a middle-class Punjabi Sikh household, when faced with the option of pursuing her studies and getting married, Nidhi chose the former. (She was a school topper.) At the prime of her career, she founded a non-profit called Esha, which started CLABIL—India's first audio library for the visually impaired—deftly balancing both. After retiring early as the director of one of the 'Big Four' companies[1] in 2015, she founded a consultancy firm.

For her, life is not a sprint; it is a marathon in which all the members of her self-team run together. She wants to excel not only as a consultant and an entrepreneur but also as a wife, a mother and an individual. She aspires to be a 'holistic hero'.

Having worked as a successful professional with companies like SAP, Cairn India, HCL and EY, Nidhi is not the kind to succumb to the stereotype that men run the show at work and women look after the family.

Nidhi and her husband, Deshant, both enjoyed highly rewarding careers. However, when their son turned 8, they decided it was necessary to devote more time to the child. They made two decisions: first, that Nidhi will become the full-time parent and will leave her job, and second, that Deshant would share a part of his salary with Nidhi as 'compensation for loss of earning'. This ensured that both of them recognized that responsibilities were shared based on their individual interests and capabilities.

---

[1]The 'Big Four' companies are Deloitte Touche Tohmatsu India Private Limited, PwC India, KPMG India Private Limited and Ernst & Young India.

Through the agreement, Nidhi ensures that her partnership with Deshant doesn't become an 'or' game, where one partner prioritizes career while the other prioritizes kin. In fact, it is an 'and' game, where the work she does contributes to her partner's professional success.

Nidhi keeps alive her financial independence through her 'and' way of partnering. Both maintain equal autonomy and dignity to live.

Another splendid part of Nidhi's life story is that she bought a house and paid off the loan before she turned 30, which was before she had her baby. This decision gave her immense confidence to invest her time and emotional energy in her marriage and parenting. Owning a place of her own gave her the confidence to pursue her other passions as well: publishing a daily online newspaper for children titled *The Children's Post*, organizing walks for the visually impaired and printing visiting cards with names in braille. Her commitment to the family and her tireless effort in the social service front deserve recognition. 'The capabilities and competence that I am building as a parent and as a social activist should enable me to update my professional experience,' says Nidhi with conviction.

She never forgets to talk about 'the housewife motivation problem' and such theories in her workshops, because she thinks that women shy away from bringing their world view to the office. Offices need to be comfortable with these metaphors, which are vital perspectives. She strongly believes that the professional excellence that one brings to the table is a reflection of our domestic life. A clear and clutter-free mind space on the domestic front helps us perform better at work.

Although Nidhi takes much pride in her career and her NGO, it is the mention of her son that makes her break into a smile and her eyes glimmer. When I met Ishaan, he was all of 10—and already an avid golfer and student of Sanskrit. At that time, he was busy preparing for his TED-Ed Talk on an antimatter universe.

Nidhi's way of partnering with her husband is a mix of romance and reality. 'In the beginning, love sustains everything else, but as we move deeper into a partnership, everything else sustains the love,' she says. Her 'poetic and pragmatic' approach to partnering spills over to the other realms of her life, making her a professional who executes with empathy and a parent who loves as well as limits it.

This 'transfer learning' improves her capabilities in various domains due to the cross-pollination of knowledge and experience.

'Cross-functional innovation helps me become a better version of myself: as a partner, a parent, a professional as well as a person,' she emphasizes as she shares her experience of being identified amongst the few internal innovators at Cairn India for an Internal Innovation Centre for cross-functional teams. What she learnt about Agile and Lean project management was applied to running her NGO, making it a uniquely successful model, where students aspire to gain internship and learn. There are no employees, only interns, at Esha; yet, it runs a unique project called Clabil (Central Library of Audio Books in Indian Languages, www.clabil.org). Esha was a case study in lean organization at the 2015 Agile Confluence—no mean feat for an NGO to achieve. She applies the same principles to managing her home and managing her time.

At the young age of 40, Nidhi has five international certifications[2] to her credit. She is already planning and preparing for an active second innings of her career and a fulfilling life thereafter. 'I want to keep all the wheels of my life lubricated till I plunge into platinum age,' she says. Planning for 'perennialling' and preparing for a second career innings are the other interesting practices of this 'work-in-progress' woman. Perennials are ever relevant people who stay energized, engaged for the longest possible age. Perennialling refers to the act of moving with the times by perennials.

Though Nidhi is an accomplished professional, a balanced partner and a passionate parent, she doesn't figure amongst those .01 per cent of people who have a Wikipedia page dedicated to them. This book is aimed at the other 99.99 per cent of the population. There is a handful of 'action takers' like Nidhi who have pivoted their life to make it wholesome, holistic and fulfilling at all times.

Let us call them 'holistic heroes', who are ready to integrate excellence in all the roles that they choose to play in life. This is practising excellence in anything and everything—excellence everywhere.

---

[2]The certificates are: SAP; SAP-HCM provided by SAP, the world's largest ERP company; PMI, provided by Project Management Institute; PMI-ACP, provided by Project Management Institute; and Complex Change Agent Certificate.

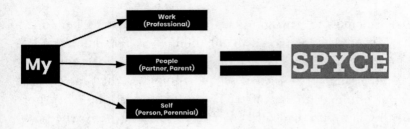

THE FIVE THINGS THAT HOLISTIC HEROES ARE DOING DIFFERENTLY

Are you a 'holistic hero' or wish to work towards becoming one? Do you wish to live a life where your success and satisfaction levels factor in the wholesomeness of your life? A quick look at the five things holistic heroes do differently will enable you to recognize, reflect and review your life goals in the long run.

1. They do not make a specific dimension of their life 'the hero' but rather focus on all the dimensions. For them, it is not enough to succeed as a professional or as a parent. They wish to excel in all the chosen 'P' roles—that of a professional, a partner, a parent and a person.

   Though teaming up all the Ps to work in sync is almost like reaching level 127 in Candy Crush, it is worth a try.

2. They wish to change the flawed script that suggests that life is an 'or' game between work and relationships, played by 'men at work' and 'women at relationships'. They wish for all partners to pursue 'career and kin' goals collectively to enjoy the quality of life that they all

deserve. Though division of domains simplifies life, it discriminates against some and dilutes the joys of life for all. What they are trying to aspire for is neither a 'fairy tale' nor a 'joy ride'. However, it is surely a 'compelling story' that needs to be written and shared.

3. Innovative thinkers and trendsetters like Nidhi are advocating 'relevance and reverence' for all the efforts exerted in various domains during the performance of various P roles.

   For them, it is not enough to merely discuss the professional perspective in boardroom meetings. Partnering and parenting as meta-skills should be measured alongside professional appraisal. Though voicing of all 'P' perspectives at critical junctures might sound like a muddled mash-up, it will improve the playlist of life in the long run.

4. Such crusaders are champions for cross-pollination of skills between various P roles. For them, it is not enough to sharpen one's knowledge as a professional. Sharing of knowledge as a partner and transferring the learnings as a parent will add to the professional expertise and vice versa. Though learning patience from a mother and emotional intelligence from a spouse is not yet popular, it is the 'dark horse' of holistic living in the coming years.

5. These people can foresee a long life, meandering into the seventies and eighties for many of us—which was not a norm earlier.

   With lives extending and relationships shrinking, a new game plan is crucial for excelling in the later years of life through perennialling.

Though we are conditioned to retire from work and life at a young age of 60, the longevity of our lives will soon push us all to embrace wholesome living till the credits start to roll on the multiplex of life.

Though planning for a second career and a joyful platinum celebration is not trending yet, it should.

You must be wondering why I am talking about trendsetters like Nidhi and suggesting the above-mentioned changes when we have been living with a social script that seems to be working for ages. I am advocating working towards rewriting our 'how-to-live' script because the science and art of living have evolved over time, particularly with the advent of technology.

Let us take an example. Our doctor inserts a digital thermometer in our mouth and looks for 98.6 degrees Fahrenheit, our normal body temperature. If it is less or more than that range, we feel stressed that something is wrong with our health. Each one of us has been treated for fever numerous times, but is our premise of normal body temperature correct? Are we following a primitively set temperature norm without bothering to investigate its veracity? This temperature titan was prescribed by Dr Carl Wunderlich in the 1850s after taking the vital signs of 25,000 patients. But he used a foot-long thermometer which was placed in the armpit, not in the mouth and which measured a temperature two degrees centigrade higher than the current thermometer.[3]

---

[3]Nguyen, Stephanie K., 'Are We Wrong About Fevers?' Medscape, 19 October 2018, www.medscape.com/viewarticle/903555. Accessed on 3 May 2022.

Dr Philip A. Mackowiak, a professor of medicine at the University of Maryland and a medical historian, conducted an experiment on healthy volunteers and found that only 8 per cent of the data set had the temperature that we have been considering normal.[4] He found the actual 'normal' temperature to be 98.2 degrees Fahrenheit. He also added other findings to establish the fact that body temperature is more like a fingerprint which is unique to bodies. Temperature varies throughout the day. Temperature goes up during the menstrual cycle for women and also when you exercise. He concluded that looking at a rise in temperature as a reliable sign of infection or disease is inappropriately simplistic thinking.

The point I am trying to make here is that all sciences, say, medical science or computer science, evolve over time. Many treatments that were followed for centuries fill the current medical practitioners with guilt as the clinical experiments have proved them to be doing absolutely the opposite of what they were supposed to be doing. Scientific discovery and research have provided evidence of how wrong we had been in treating measles without antibiotics, or putting stents in the hearts when not needed.

Similarly, the science of 'living' has evolved. Various cultural, psychological and medical improvements have changed the way we lead our lives. Yet, a majority of us wish to believe the ossified orders of previous centuries regarding personal happiness, holistic excellence, gender equality and lifestyle transformation.

---

[4]Stroh, Michael, 'A Baltimore researcher shows that the longtime standard for body temperature is wrong. Cool', *The Baltimore Sun*, 11 February 2005, https://bit.ly/3Nmbw53. Accessed on 16 May 2022.

We have better access to the crevices of our brain. We study data better—given the resources at our disposal. We spend our time and effort on entirely different things than what we were two decades ago. So, we need a new script for a personal reform, a familial restructuring, a social re-engineering and a cultural refurbishing.

Let me answer the 'whys' around all the desired changes mentioned above before getting into the 'whats' and the 'hows'. In this context, the first question is: why excelling in a single dimension, i.e. work, family or self, is no longer enough?

In his book *How Will You Measure Your Life?* Clayton M. Christensen, the Harvard Business School expert on innovation, shares the story of his Harvard days.[5] When he met his classmates on their fifth-year reunion, most of them were happy and successful, climbing the ladder of professional success and starting families. Some of them didn't show up for the tenth reunion. Some of them seemed discontent although they were working with Fortune 500 companies. Christensen realized that for many of them, while their professional lives blossomed, their personal lives plummeted. There was a striking contrast between the trajectories of their personal and professional lives. And the worst part was that he noticed a constant deterioration in their mental well-being all the way through to the twenty-fifth and thirtieth reunions. He saw the same 'personal dissatisfaction, family failures, professional struggles, and

---

[5]Christensen, Clayton M., *How Will You Measure Your Life?,* Harper Business, 2012.

even criminal behaviour' in his Rhodes Scholars batch at Oxford University too.[6] He realized that these professional climbers were not happy being who they were despite being the 'best educated' and 'best employed' of the lot.

This deterioration happens when we focus on excelling in one dimension alone during our formative years. We are taught to prepare solely for professional success, while our family becomes more like a shadow, lurking in the background. Not only have we been tutored to scale professional heights, we have also been programmed to idolize and emulate those who achieve unprecedent success at work. Our role models usually are those who have succeeded professionally, invented new products, created terrific films or touched the lives of many.

We, as a society, overvalue and overemphasize professional accomplishments. We never bother about how these achievers fare as individuals, sans their professional accomplishments. We think it's enough for a person to excel in one P of their life while faring disappointingly in the other realms.

We are encouraged to be like Arjuna and develop the kind of focus he had, oblivious to the whirlwind of the world around him. As important as focus is in our life, doesn't a steadfast and rigid focus like that entail missing out on all that the beautiful world has to offer? Arjuna perhaps never felt the breeze on his face or marvelled at the colours of the bird's wings, in other words, never enjoyed the simpler pleasures of life. This leads us to the question: what did Arjuna gain by being so focussed? He felt completely helpless in the

[6]Ibid. 7.

Mahabharata war, when he needed his prowess the most.

Also, what did Arjuna lose by being so focussed? Archery occupied his complete being. He was perhaps clueless about life apart from archery, the same way we find professionals today being clueless about life apart from their quarterly results.

We worship charismatic leaders who dazzle in the realms of sports, business, films, science or other sectors without observing how inspiring they are as parents, partners or people.

Giving undue and excessive importance to one dimension of our heroes' lives, putting them on a pedestal is doing a disservice to them as well as to ourselves. It is unfair to the heroes as they, too, start believing in that pedestal as the ultimate reality and start making unrealistic demands from everyone around them. They start having unrealistic expectations from themselves too, which usually results in dejection and disappointment.

Majority of people allow their jobs to wreak havoc in their life as they are consumed by jealousy over another's professional rise. They let their marriages die as they slog in those wretched jobs. They decide to have a child in that dead marriage, becoming a 'cold' parent.

Hence, I wish to script a new way of life where we set ourselves up for excellence in 'all' that we do.

Let us not dream of becoming a part of the 4 Comma Club but work to infuse excellence in all spheres of our life.

Vinay Lal, a historian at University of California, Los Angeles (UCLA), talks about the obsession Indians have with setting records, as bizarre as having the maximum number of tattoos or having the world's longest fingernails.

People crave for social validation and are ready to walk the extra mile in search of an 'icon' status—so what if it is of a Facebook group?[7] Such fixation with being merely a successful professional or an FB icon is equivalent to thinking that as long as I have an excellent heart, I am fine with weak kidneys and a suboptimal liver.

There was a time in the twentieth century when rigid specialization was a norm—it being an offshoot of the Industrial Revolution. Now is the time to not separate work and play, it's all living. (Thanks, Richard Branson, for saying it.)

Why should we chase professional achievement leaving behind our partnerial, parental and personal journeys? Why should we focus only on the parental realm while not paying enough attention to the rest? Let us not sprint with one P while the other Ps wait for a tomorrow that never comes.

The second desired change that Nidhi's story brings forth is to change the gender-based equation that constitutes a family. The question that needs an answer is: why on earth am I pressing for an 'and' game between partners when an 'or' game has been the norm? Let us understand why this change is needed. Life today resembles a swimrun championship rather than a swimming or running competition. The Swimrun World Championship is an expedition challenging nature and time both, where two teams swim and run together for a stretch of 75 kilometres in a day (10 kilometres are open-water swimming and 65 kilometres are trail-running). The team members cannot be farther than 10 metres from

[7]Lal, Vinay, 'Indians and the Guinness Book of Records', UCLA Social Sciences MANAS, https://bit.ly/3y6jquQ. Accessed on 3 May 2022.

each other anytime during the race. Both *run* in their wetsuits and *swim* with their shoes on—the way we need to cope in life sometimes without changing gear. Despite severe hardships, 148 out of the 160 teams that participated in the 2018 world championship finished the race.[8] When life can be a swim as well as a run, living a narrow life primarily as a professional or a parent is limiting the possibilities that life offers.

Also, we need to break stereotypes like: 'When the husband is earning enough, why does the wife need to work?' or 'A married couple must have children' or 'A mother who holds on to her career alongside her children is selfish and aggressive'. We need a social re-engineering of our thoughts about expectations from men and women within marriage and family and also outside of it.

Our current social script has written the character of a man to be career-centric and that of a woman to be family-centric. This script gives the power to the person who earns and runs the show outside the boundaries of home. Even when a woman earns, she is expected to fulfil all her domestic responsibilities. On the contrary, a man can choose to shoulder domestic responsibilities, but he is not expected to. He is accepted and expected to be incompetent in the domestic domain. A woman is allowed to work professionally till the other roles of partner and parent are absent. Being permanently tagged as a primary caregiver, she remains kin-centric and the man of the house enjoys the 'career-centric' status. This is a lopsided view. Both deserve to share the load as well as enjoy the benefits, on the personal and professional front.

---

[8]'ÖTILLÖ, The Swimrun World Championship – Race Directors Report 2018', https://bit.ly/3MnOI4D. Accessed on 16 May 2022.

A career-centric man and a kin-centric woman miss out on quality of life which they deserve to enjoy by pursuing 'career and kin' goals collectively.

A man desires and deserves to be an involved husband, a present father and a warm person apart from being a busy professional. Our cultural stereotypes have given him a mask of masculinity owing to which he sees power in earning money and acquiring status, not in feeling loved and needed.

A woman, on the other hand, desires and deserves to be a high-performing professional and a powerful person apart from being a loving spouse and a nurturing mother. Our cultural stereotypes have given her a halo of being this self-sacrificing persona owing to which she sees meaning in being generous and kind, not in seeking power of position and professional excellence.

Let man and woman not divide their roles and dilute the quality of their experiences.

Let them come together and create a synergy between their 'internal teams' to live more meaningful lives. Every man and woman should go all out and live their lives in full throttle where both enjoy equal autonomy and a dignity to live.

Many of us would predictably argue that everyone trying to earn a dime and run a family is an unnecessary struggle. Martha Nussbaum, a professor of law and ethics at The University of Chicago, explains these practical and moral conflicts of daily life using Greek mythological stories. She talks about Agamemnon, a Greek king who was leading his army to Troy. Suddenly, his expedition was halted as the gods demanded a sacrifice of his daughter to complete the expedition. He faced two deep and entirely legitimate commitments coming into a terrible conflict.[9] Nussbaum juxtaposes this big dilemma with our daily dilemma of juggling our career and being a good parent. She says that both enrich each other and make the life of each of them better. However, everyday problems do arise; for instance, an important meeting at work might coincide with your child's performance at school or a PTM. When faced with such a situation, we have to make a choice depending on what our priorities are. And in the process, one of your priorities will suffer, not because you are an incompetent leader or a bad parent but because such is life, and such is the tragedy of life.

To avoid this daily conflict, you might opt out of leadership (since it is not possible to stop being a parent). You perhaps want to avoid a daily conflict, a daily tragedy. So, you turn the 'full-life' into a 'half-life' and start concentrating on that 'half-life' more to make it seem full. Also, when we are capable as a leader but are unable to do full justice to our role, it is a constant reminder that we have not reached our full potential.

So, you decide to exit it completely. We make that choice essentially because we fear being judged by society for nurturing the desire to become a leader as much as being a parent. We are afraid of being tagged as 'ambitious' (yes, that has negative connotations). We are scared of being judged as someone who does not prioritize their family.

Sociologist and bestselling author Malcolm Gladwell

---

[9]'Martha Nussbaum: Applying the Lessons of Ancient Greece', BillMoyers.com, 16 November 1988, https://billmoyers.com/content/martha-nussbaum/. Accessed on 3 May 2022.

defines capitalization rate of human potential as 'the rate at which a given community capitalizes on the human potential'.[10] If a person has the potential to be a 10, but in reality, is a 2, his capitalization will be 10/2. Gladwell points out three main reasons for the low capitalization rates of human potential: poverty, stupidity and culture.

Most people fail to use their holistic potential due to lack of resources, when institutions come in their way or when our cultural notions encourage us not to excel.

Here, I am advocating to play the 'and' game so that the capitalization rate of female potential increases followed by an overall increase in the capitalization rate of human potential. If the current rate is low, we should improve it. Reducing poverty is out of the scope of this book, but we surely can cut down our collective stupidity and social stereotyping by bringing the change from 'boys fix things and girls need things fixed' to 'boys and girls fix things that they need'.

Another question that needs an answer to is: why is it not advisable to 'spotlight' only one aspect of your personality? For example, 'workplace spotlighting' the performance of a sales manager without paying any attention to his actions as a community leader, or 'family spotlighting' the culinary prowess of a woman who is also an influencer. To answer the why behind it, we need to realize the urgent need of 'wholesomeness' in our lives.

A firm cannot be at the top of its game if the finance

[10]'Malcolm Gladwell Explains Why Human Potential Is Being Squandered [PopTech Video]', *Mutual Responsibility*, https://bit.ly/3N4ddUD. Accessed on 3 May 2022.

department excels while the production department merely floats and the human resources department is fainting on the way. Similarly, a person cannot be at his best if the 'professional in him' dances to glory while the 'partner in him' drudges in a corner.

Parenting cannot be seen as a so-called gap on the résumé any more. It is a set of skills that makes us better professionals and better people. A successful marriage or a functional family, which is becoming rarer, needs to be valued and given its due position in measuring the quality of life.

Acknowledging and aligning all the 'P' perspectives will bring 'working' and 'living' closer. Consequently, workplaces will become more human. Moreover, people (both men and women) who stay at home to take care of their children or elders should ideally get a smooth re-entry into the workforce, without being judged. Both are challenging responsibilities and should not be looked down upon just because it does not come with a pay package.

On searching online, we find several deathbed regrets. We only have such lists for men. There is no such list available online describing deathbed regrets of women. Ridiculous, but true.

The realms in which women are expected to excel are not given the importance they deserve outside the home. Partnerial and parental skills are considered 'lowlights' and professional skills are considered 'highlights'. All the work that goes into raising a family, sustaining a marriage, fostering self-improvement and taking care of the people who need it the most cannot remain just a side dish on the plate of life.

Let us try to understand this difference with the help of an example. Anaesthesia was discovered in Boston's Massachusetts General Hospital and, within two months, it became a regularly used tool in hospitals across several nations, as it provided immediate relief and people didn't need to wait to see its valuable impact.

It happened for two reasons:

a) It gave relief immediately. People didn't need to wait to see its valuable impact, and

b) It not only helped patients but also was a boon for doctors as it reduced patients screaming on the operation table.

However, another medical discovery, antiseptics, was not in much prevalence even after decades, despite its utility, as the benefits took some time to show. Also, the initial use of antiseptics was cumbersome for doctors.[11] To put it simply, people take time and some effort to take to those things that show positive effect only after a lapse of time. They instead swear by things that give a positive result immediately. Being a professional gives an immediate positive result, the most important aspect being that you get paid every month. Being a partner and a parent causes some amount of pain and a sense of discomfort in the initial stages and holds the promise of gain/benefits later. That is why most of us intend to work on professional excellence at the cost of partnerial and parental excellence.

---

[11]Gawande, Atul, 'Spreading Slow Ideas', *The New Yorker*, 10 July 2019, www.newyorker.com/magazine/2013/07/29/slow-ideas. Accessed on 4 May 2022.

Just like antiseptics did not impact the lives of doctors and patients as much as anaesthesia, partnerial and parental responsibilities did not impact the lives of men as much as professional responsibilities. Hence, doctors did not have an immediate affinity for antiseptics and men did not show a natural inclination to familial roles. However, it is clear that medical excellence needs to give equal importance to anaesthesia and antiseptics and excellence 360 degree needs to give equal importance to all the P roles that we have discussed so far.

Since the meaningfulness of our life doesn't depend only on becoming an 'envy-inducing professional' or an 'in-line partner', but rather on our 'wholesomeness' as an individual, we need to take all the P perspectives to the finish line.

Let us acknowledge all the perspectives of an individual— as a perennial and professional, as a partner, a parent and a person. After acknowledging these experiences, let us align them in a way that we are able to capitalize the full potential of each. Acknowledging and aligning our partnering and parenting skills will turn them into meta-skills, which is as valuable as professional experience accumulated over the years.

A desired change that people like Nidhi and I wish to bring about is the cross-pollination of knowledge across various P roles. Let me answer why we need to stimulate all the roles by transferring takeaways from one domain to another.

It was not possible earlier to have cross-functional knowledge as people lived unidimensional, suboptimal, divided lives. Now that we are pioneering a personal disruption by integrating an internal team of professional, partner, parent and person, knowledge sharing and transfer learning across roles is not only possible but much needed.

Each person has an 'internal team', so to say, within. Knowledge sharing between various roles at this micro level is a key change that is needed. The cross-functional exchange of skills will strengthen the existing ones and add some new competencies to the internal team. Simply put, 'the parent in me' can transfer learnings to the 'professional in me' and the 'partner in me' can pick up new competencies from the 'professional in me'. Therefore, it is a win-win situation for both parties.

If a father cultivates the virtue of patience while taking care of his newborn, transfer learning happens when he is able to take the feedback of his team more patiently and without losing his cool.

Again, if an entrepreneur opens up and is vulnerable in front of his partner, the same learning can be transferred to his role as a spouse wherein his 'opening up' addresses trust issues, leading to a better bonding between the two life partners.

Enabling the transfer of learning from the parent, partner and personal realms will have two positive impacts. First, the professional realms will be enriched by these learnings. Second, the time and energy spent in excelling as a partner, a parent and a person will get its due. In fact, I suggest incorporating a 'P' index in the 'knowledge' dimension of human development index, which at present, merely uses an education index to measure the knowledge of a nation. This 'education index' sadly counts the mean of years of schooling to measure the knowledge base of a person. This one-dimensional emphasis on school/

college education makes us a multi-loser. First, we stop considering anything that we add to our knowledge base after finishing college as 'learning'. Second, we stop learning altogether outside of classrooms. While professionals collect certifications and take up courses online, they never look at learnings from other realms as 'knowledge' translating into wisdom for life. Thus, a 'P' index and marking these meta-skills as 'soft talents' can make partnering, parenting and personal skills measurable, thus leading to measurable learning outcomes.

Think of Brazilian soccer players who have five World Cup victories under their belt. Players like Pelé and Ronaldinho, among others, were used to playing a game in childhood called futsal. This is a strange game, where the ball is half the size of a football but weighs double. The playground is the size of a football court and each side has five to six players. This game improves ball control, vision and speed of passing the ball. These skills, when transferred to football, make Brazilians unmatchable.

The Canadian-American mathematician Manjul Bhargava owes his mathematical intelligence to his penchant for music. The cross-pollination between Fibonacci numbers and tabla beats has helped him excel at both.[12]

If futsal skills can improve football skills and music skills can fire up mathematic skills, then parenting skills can surely improve professional skills and vice versa.

Let knowledge sharing and transfer learning help us in

---

[12]Klarreich, Erica, 'The Musical, Magical Number Theorist', *Quanta Magazine*, 12 August 2014, https://bit.ly/3ycokGx. Accessed on 4 May 2022.

excelling in not one role, but different roles that we play in life.[13]

The final change championed by Nidhi's story is consistent planning to excel in the latter part of our lives. The question then is: why do we need a rigorous plan for our platinum years?

Well, the answer is both profound and practical. Profound because we all deserve to lead a content and fulfilling life till the end and the practical reason is our increasing life expectancy and decreasing family support. People need to think about extending their careers or pursuing a second career after investing heavily in parental and partnerial roles.

Nidhi and many like her are crafting their careers after 40 and 50 years of age to work meaningfully for the next 25 years. In fact, *New York Times* bestselling author Chip Conley calls on us to treat age as we would other types of diversity. These 'modern elders', as he calls them, will rewrite the definition of ageing and geriatrics.[14]

Dr Vibha Tripathi, 53, co-founder and managing director of Swajal Water—a multi-award-winning Internet of Things (IoT)-enabled water-purification solutions provider—has a PhD in physics from the Indian Institute of Technology (IIT) Kanpur.[15] She is one of those who passed out of a reputed

---

[13]Coyle, Daniel, 'The Sweet Spot', in *The Talent Code: Greatness Isn't Born. It's Grown, Here's How,* Arrow, 2010, pp. 24–29.

[14]Conley, Chip, *Wisdom at Work: The Making of a Modern Elder, How to Reinvent the Second Half of Your Career,* Portfolio Penguin, 2018.

[15]Balachandran, Manu, 'Meet Swajal, the Startup That's Quenching the Thirst of the Needy', *Forbes India*, 29 August 2018, https://bit.ly/3kE8M6M. Accessed on 4 May 2022.

educational institute almost 25 years ago but is making a mark now.

She has partnered with her son Advait, an electrical engineer from Pennsylvania State University, for her water project. The intellectual and emotional power of such women will shape a new social set-up where everyone can strive to contribute to their fullest. In India, female professionals are mostly lone family warriors as their husbands are raised to advance their careers, and women, despite being educated and professionally experienced, are normally expected to put in their papers at the altar of their family. Through this change, I intend to dignify dotage. I hope that it will encourage everyone to plan and prepare for old age from their midlife onwards so that they can stay healthy and stimulated after crossing the fence of youth.

These five desired changes form the root of this book. These changes, if brought about, will create excellence 360 degree. This book propagates excellence 360 degree through a concept called SPYCE: Sum of a Person, Partner, Parent, Professional and Perennial in You to Create Excellence. This concept is born out of my interactions, contemplation, discussions and reflections in the last five years around achieving excellence 360 degree throughout life. SPYCE is a multidimensional acknowledgement of excellence in our lives, a well-rounded appreciation of our lives. This book will take you on a journey to create your own SPYCE to live a life infused with excellence 360 degree.

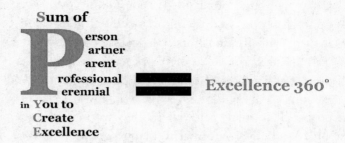

Sum of Person Partner Parent Professional Perennial in You to Create Excellence = Excellence 360°

The next five chapters will build the five pillars of SPYCE on which excellence 360 degree will be enthroned.

Chapter 2 conceptualizes the first principle 'Self-Teaming' by encouraging each one of us to become holistic heroes. It will provide all the practical tips on how to form a 'self-team' while stressing that it is perfectly fine if you wish not to don all the 'P' hats. 'Self-Teaming' helps each one of us to acknowledge their person, partner, professional and parent pods within and then collaborate with each one of them with agility and cohesion. Pullela Gopichand, a former Indian badminton player, is one such 'self-teamer' whose life is enthused with excellence.

Chapter 3 conceptualizes 'And Gaming' by emboldening each one of us to become 'gender agnostic'. 'And Gaming' entitles every man and woman not to divide their responsibilities but to hyphenate them so that each gets equal autonomy and dignity to live, learn, love and laugh.

Onler Kom, partner of boxing legend Mary Kom, is one such 'and gamer' par excellence.

In addition, the chapter will also provide all the practical tips on how to eschew the 'or game' and embrace the 'and game'.

Chapter 4 conceptualizes 'P Pedestalling' by energizing each one of us to give due importance to all the realms that we are a part of. It also offers practical tips on how to show up with the 'family face' at the workplace and how to create a 'P' index as a subset of the human development index. 'P Pedestalling' will enable us to make all the roles primarily played by all humans relevant so that women do not lose out professionally by primarily being parents and men do not lose out emotionally by primarily being professionals.

Satya Nadella, the executive chairman and CEO of Microsoft, is a crusader for 'P Pedestalling' as he shows up in his chairman's chamber every day with empathy he has developed as a father.

Chapter 5 conceptualizes the fourth pillar of excellence 360 degree: 'Transfer Learning' by segregating internal transfer learning and external transfer learning. The P pods of the self-team of an individual learn from each other cohesively before the external cross-functional transfer happens. My professional pod passes on some dedication to my partner pod before I, as an author, learn the art of detachment from a monk.

The American billionaire investor and hedge fund manager Ray Dalio champions the process of cross-pollination of learning with radical transparency and enables us to excel without an ego and biases.

The final chapter foretells the advent of 'Perennialling'. It encourages each one of us to plan for a dignified dotage from midlife itself so that we can take the necessary steps to lead an energetic and engaged life till the curtain call.

The Austrian-American management consultant,

educator and author Peter F. Drucker pioneered the thought of a second career late in life and implemented it, along with his wife, who founded a start-up at the age of 82.

If we only live once, why live like an incomplete piece of art? If it is possible to take all our self-team members: the professional, the partner and the parent to the podium, why settle for only one?

When we can achieve professional as well as personal greatness, why compromise for only one?

We need to motivate all the internal team members simultaneously and spontaneously which means that unidimensional specialization is not the key, multidimensional excellence is. I, as a person, need to make all my internal team members excel. You, as a person, need to do the same.

Tell the professional in you to not ignore the partner inside or let the parent lay dormant. Tell the partner in you to keep upgrading the professional aspect and prepare the parent in you for the future. Tell the parent in you to respect the professional and love the partner in you. You might say that it is a fastidious feat or a hard nut to crack. Well, the truth is, it is. But it is not impossible, especially in this day and age. Pursuing holistic personal excellence is a worthy life goal. People are conditioned to become 'big giants'—own a big company, earn a hefty package, run a big campaign or pitch a big idea.

We never prepare ourselves to have a team of small giants within us who might propel us to become a big giant but would propel us to be a happy and fulfilled small giant, for sure.

SELF-TEAMING

THE WOMAN WHO BURIED HER DREAMS TO REALIZE THEM

A girl in rural Zimbabwe was exchanged for a cow at the age of 11 and was forced to marry an abusive older man. She never went to school but learned to read and write by helping her brother with his homework. She was a mother to four even before she turned 18. At the time when she was pregnant for the fourth time, an American woman named Jo Luck had come to her village for community work and on seeing her condition, asked her about her dreams. To which she replied that she wanted to go to the US, get an undergraduate degree, a master's and PhD and come back and work for her community.[16]

---

[16]Mbugua, Sam, et al., 'Tererai Trent: Awaken to Your Full Potential

She confided her dreams in two women: the American social worker who came to her village and her mother. Jo Luck inspired her to go for her dreams and her mother asked her to write her dreams on a piece of paper and bury them in the ground. This was a ritual in rural Zimbabwe, a way of making sure your dreams came true. Imagine a woman who is barely literate, extremely poor, a wife and a mother at that, raring to achieve what seemed almost impossible at that point. This, however, is the real life story of Tererai Trent, the Zimbabwean-American educator who became the most favourite guest of Oprah Winfrey on her iconic talk show.

Tererai permitted herself to dream of a life that was strikingly in contrast with the one she had. She believed that living in her village was like a relay race, where a baton of poverty was handed over by her great-grandmother to her grandmother, who passed it on to her mother and eventually to her. But she was not okay with that. So, she changed the race and the rules to run.

It took her eight years to finish her high school diploma from Cambridge through correspondence before she got admitted to Oklahoma State University in 1998. She could have gone to the US alone and sent money back home for the family but she knew that her children would be married off in her absence, as happened with her. So, when her husband refused to let go of the children, she brought the whole family with her, including him. Her steely resolve helped her put food on the table and pay the tuition fees.

---

and Achieve the Impossible', *Lewis Howes*, 1 February 2018, https://bit.ly/3sbLs49. Accessed on 4 May 2022.

They lived in a trailer. She partnered with people and sought their help. She asked her university for assistance when she could not pay her tuition fee. At one point when she was going through a rough patch financially, she was asked to buy stale food from the local store! However, some people shared her enthusiasm and trusted her as they could see her ambition and dedication, not only to her dreams but to her family as well.

Since Tererai knew about agriculture given her rural background, she mastered in plant pathology and started working with the NGO Heifer International, which was involved in eradicating poverty and hunger through sustainable, values-based holistic community development. Her authenticity, ambition and creativity strengthened her to create a shared context with others. It was at this time that Tererai was invited to the *Oprah Winfrey Show*, where Oprah made a donation of $1.5 billion to rebuild schools in Zimbabwe. The Tererai Trent International, in partnership with Oprah Winfrey and 'Save the children', has built 11 schools in Zimbabwe, which cater to more than 5,000 children.

This is not the life story of an unusual woman, this is the story of a 'holistic hero' who was ready to be everything— from a child bride and battered wife to a creative student, a dependable mother and a community builder.

She never looked for perfection in any role or realm, she took baby steps for two decades to be good enough in every role and realm. Her P pods teamed up with agility allowing her to think swiftly and simultaneously like a student, as a professional, a parent and a partner. She lived with the wrong 'fits' of an abusive husband but never hesitated to look for the 'right fit' professionally and personally. After her abusive husband was deported in 2003, she married her fellow plant pathologist Mark Trent. Her self-team anchored her never-ending journey and enabled her to never surrender to the social script or the cultural stereotypes. Tererai acknowledged and embraced all the P pods of her self-team with self-belief and she continues to march ahead without neglecting any of the pods.

WHAT IS SELF-TEAMING?

Each one of us gets into various roles during our lifespan. These roles are played by a congregation of P pods—person, professional, partner and parent—stationed inside us, waiting to be acknowledged, catalysed and prepared, at the appropriate time based on how we decide to live. We all possess within us four pods—person, professional, partner and parent—which can be acknowledged, catalysed and prepared, sequentially or simultaneously, before searching for an external fit.

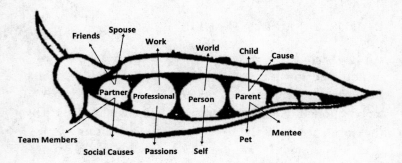

We cannot think of working for any corporation or cause without working internally on the professional pod. We should not partner with allies or a spouse without internally preparing the partner pod. We cannot become happy and effective parents unless our parent pod evolves. These four pods make up our self-team which helps us in creating a 'self-definition' of ourselves. Apple co-founder Steve Jobs believed that people do not always know what they want. Similarly, people do not always know what all they possess. They are unaware of the self-team at their disposal.

Excellence 360 degree reminds us to make full use of the self-team from the early years. The partner pod prepares itself to partner excellently with the complete 'relationship' domain: siblings, friends, relatives, colleagues, social ties, social causes and the life partner. The professional pod prepares itself to perform excellently with the entire 'action' domain: work, side hustles, hobbies and passions. The parent pod prepares itself to grow excellently with the 'seeking' domain: causes, followers, mentees, pets, old parents and children. The person pod prepares itself to live excellently with oneself and the world.

HOW TO BE A SELF-TEAMER

A self-teamer is an agile shape-shifter who leads a multidimensional life on a daily basis. They build an inner infrastructure which is not 'perfect' for a specific domain but 'good enough' for all the domains. They consistently strive for excellence in all the roles, believing in continuity, rather than beginnings or endings. This is how it can be done:

Preparing the congregation of Ps: The easiest way to solve a problem is to deny that it exists, said the American writer Isaac Asimov. That is what we do by choosing a unidimensional life that doesn't acknowledge the presence of all the Ps inside us. A self-teamer brings about the change by following these steps:

1. **Acknowledge the Ps:** One cannot start on a weight-loss journey unless they acknowledge that the problem of obesity is real. Self-teaming is not possible unless one acknowledges all the P pods that need equal attention and catalysing. Let all the Ps sign up for a fulfilling life.

   A universal question every toddler is asked is what they want to be when they grow up. The expected answer is 'a doctor' or 'an astronaut', perhaps. An acknowledgement of different Ps would mean creating a social script where the answer would be something like, 'I want to be a doctor, a dad and an optimist guy' or 'I want to become an astronaut and a mom'. Acknowledging a full self-team is like mouthing a rational but radical idea which needs social courage.

   School curriculums and family behaviours can build this courage and instil this confidence by introducing the possibility of a multidimensional life for children. Acknowledging all the Ps means a transition, from being a hero to a holistic hero. A hero is someone who does something beyond the ordinary, who gives life to something or someone bigger than oneself.[17] A holistic

---

[17]Campbell, Joseph, *The Hero with a Thousand Faces*, Yogi Impressions, 2017; Rank, Otto, *Myth of the Birth of the Hero: A Psychological Exploration*

hero is someone who moves beyond ordinariness in all the chosen roles and realms to live an excellence-infused multidimensional life.

A hero performs two types of deeds: a physical deed of heroism, like saving a life or a spiritual deed of heroism, like transforming a life. A holistic hero, on the other hand, saves his own life every day from the drudgery of a unidimensional existence tethered to perfection. He transforms himself every day into a team of happy and fulfilled small giants rather than a unidimensional giant. Acknowledging the congregation of Ps is acknowledging the complete self-team which introduces the concept of holistic heroism in our cultural fabric.

A hero undergoes 'conscious transformation' which strengthens him to take the tough path of departure-fulfilment-return. Every life begins with the heroic act of birth where the water creature in the womb transforms into a breathing mammal. However, a holistic hero follows a constant path of moving to and fro between various chosen roles. There is neither a permanent departure nor a permanent return. There is a fluid flow between different professional and personal realms all the time. Acknowledging the whole set of Ps requires solitude—not being alone, but being more intimately connected with oneself. It requires diving deep into oneself to tie in with all the Ps before enhancing social ties.

We can look up to an individual like Sudha Murty, businesswoman, educator, author and philanthropist,

of Myth, Johns Hopkins University Press, 2015.

who seems to be a holistic hero, gliding effortlessly and silently between various P pods. Her 'person' pod made her an authentic and creative student who catalysed her ambition, acumen and dedication before applying for a professional position at Telco. Her courage compelled the Tata group to rethink their hiring policy for women, and she became the first woman engineer to be hired at the Pune site of Telco. The 'partner' pod of her self-team was so well-prepared that she partnered with Narayan Murty to not only start a family but also a new company. She shared the context of building a new company and a new life with her husband and readily chose to not be a part of Infosys when her husband was clear that only one of them could be a part of the company. Her agility, humour and observation have always been on point, making her a much-loved author, mother and mentor.

2. **Ask the right questions and activate the ready Ps:** The 'person' pod should first ask questions to know its own core. Answering these questions will enable the 'person' pod to know oneself and gauge one's growth. One could ask questions like:

What moves me the most as a human? (A beggar/A Mercedes-Benz)

What do I love the most in myself? (Looks/Intelligence/Inheritance)

How do I face failure, criticism and emotional setbacks?

When will I catalyse my next P Pod?

As the 'person' pod engages in some *self-talk*, it would figure out which P pod needs the catalysing next. Further questioning would help in finding out the next P pod that needs activation. Some sample questions could be like:

What makes one look forward to the next day? (A high-five from a friend/Dad's approval/Grades)

What do I want to ignore right now? (A risk/An argument/Staying alone)

Based on the answers, the new pod will be activated. If the 'partner' pod gets the nod for activation from the 'person' pod, the 'person' pod will ensure that the new pod has a good time from the beginning. Both should continue to grow and collaborate with each other without envy.

Each P pod has the following seeds inside:

Person Pod	*Partner Pod*	*Professional Pod*	*Parent Pod*
Authenticity	Shared Context	Ambition	Persuasion
Creativity	Power Balance	Acumen	Egolessness
Humility	Love	Commitment	Observation

(All these seeds are explained in detail in Chapter 5.)

These seeds remain available to all of us. We can pick and peel them, polish them and put them to good use. We can also choose to not pay attention to some of them. In that case, the unattended Ps will lose their lustre.

Activating these pods means putting them to use. We sometimes rush into forming a relationship without preparing our own pod. Investor and innovator Daymond

John agreed that he rushed into marriage and fatherhood. Without catalysing his own partner and parent pods, he could never give his family the love, nurturing, time and attention that they needed and deserved.

A list of suggested questions is given at the end of the book which various pods should be asking themselves to improve their competence in the self-team.

3. **Recalibrate the rhythm with new activation:** With the activation of a new P Pod inside the self-team, an inner recalibration is needed. For different individuals, the activation and recalibration will be different. For instance, a 14-year-old boy is being raised by ambitious parents and hence, it is only the professional pod which has been activated. Now, the boy realizes that he needs to explore his personality. After acknowledging the presence of the other three pods, he activates the person pod alongside the professional pod. Ambition and acumen of the boy make some place for creativity and authenticity. The new seeds start communicating and the one-dimensional approach changes to two-dimensional. At 18, he decides to catalyse the partner pod when he participates in an exhibition with his friends. Their idea gets attention and encouragement. The 18-year-old activates the 'partner' pod of his self-team to prepare himself internally before getting into any external partnership. The pods recalibrate their equation by inviting seeds of love and trust. All the pods need equal space and importance in the self-team after activation.

With the pods' positioning in the self-team, the 'texture' of the self-team starts shaping up. The sooner the pods get activated, the better equipped we become to live a multidimensional life. No one pod is enough to give us fulfilment. Our professional pod might give us riches and accomplishments, our person pod might give us an authentic, unique identity, but the addition of partner and parent pod will give us emotional strength and reasons to approach each day with zeal and vigour.

4. **Infuse agility, burstiness and cohesion:** With the activation of various pods, the self-team needs an infusion of agility, burstiness and cohesion. Agility is the ability to think, understand and move, quickly. A self-teamer needs to learn to manoeuvre quickly between different pods with ease so that an individual can meditate, negotiate a deal, wipe a tear and dance in the rain in the same day. Agility will enable all the P pods to stay racy and relevant. Agility will empower one to fulfil their career and kin goals and to integrate work and life better.

Burstiness is the backbone of any creative and innovative team. A self-team infused with burstiness will have mutual respect between all P pods, an openness that will lower their inhibitions and welcome criticism from each other. Burstiness will enable all the members of the self-team to know which P pod needs priority in a particular situation.[18]

Cohesion is the sticking together of particles of the same substance. A self-team will be cohesive like a peloton—a formation made by a team of cyclists which

[18]Ketel, Jerry, '"Burstiness" for the most innovative teams', Medium.com, https://bit.ly/3kExV11. Accessed on 4 May 2022.

reduces air resistance and helps the team of cyclists to move ahead without even pedalling. Transfer learning between various members of the self-team makes life more integrated and dignified for every gender and ethnicity. Thus, to become a 'self-teamer', one needs to acknowledge all the four P pods, activate them, recalibrate the rhythm and infuse A, B and C—agility, burstiness and cohesion—among all pods.

Preparing the P pods for excellence, not perfection: Most societies have their own distinct templates of an ideal life for a man and an ideal life for a woman. This template expects them to be perfect, in other words, following the set norms to the maximum. This safe, sensible and stable life expects every man and woman to run carefully enough that they tackle each stepping stone. This social script expects men to be perfect professionals and women to be perfect homemakers. But a self-teamer believes in excellence, not perfection.

Perfection puts only one or two P pods on the pedestal, while excellence teaches us to expand ourselves in all realms. Perfection is control. Excellence is spontaneous. Perfection is fear. Excellence is risk worth taking. Hence, a self-teamer believes in multidimensional excellence, i.e. excellence 360 degree.

It is believed that people who value perfectionism are less likely to have satisfying relationships. When a reporter asked chess grandmaster Bobby Fischer what his life would have been like had he not been so obsessed with chess, Fischer replied, 'Well, it would have been better, you know. A little more balanced...a little more rounded.'[19]

Life doesn't want us to be only an excellent athlete or an excellent musician or an excellent surgeon. Life wants us to be an excellent human being, which means excellent at living, learning, loving and laughing with the chosen P pods in tow.

Create Internal alignment and External fit: The self-team pods evolve and align themselves. The person pod works on becoming authentic, creative and humble, while the professional pod polishes his acumen, ambition and commitment. Hollywood actor Arnold Schwarzenegger says that he focuses so deeply on his muscle during a workout that he almost 'develops' a mind inside the biceps. Now that is focus!

Our P pods should have the same focussed involvement before connecting with an external fit. For example: my partner pod should be evolved and aligned enough before looking for an external bond. Unless the pod is prepared to believe in shared context, love, and a balance of power and love, no external relationship can flourish. The aim of the alignment is to:

- Be the professional you would want to hire.
- Be the partner you would want to live with.
- Be the parent you would want to have.
- Be the person you would want to emulate.

When our self-team is well-evolved and well-aligned, the

---

[19]Barker, Eric, *Barking up the Wrong Tree: The Surprising Science behind Why Everything You Know about Success Is (Mostly) Wrong*, HarperOne, 2019.

external relationships fit well and the transition is seamless. In the podcast 'Masters of Scale' by Reid Hoffman, the theme of the episode, the advertisement content and its spot are integrated so well that no interruption is felt. In an episode, the co-founder of Instagram Kevin Systrom spoke about how he created Instagram by 'keeping it simple'. The episode was suitably sponsored by the Mastercard Center for Inclusive Growth which shared the story of a simple innovation called 'doorstep banking' by the underprivileged women of an Indian village Satara in Maharashtra. The three ad spots narrated the story and it fitted comfortably with Kevin's journey. What a fluid fit!

There should be no hurry to get into an internal–external bond unless it fits well. Scott Belsky founded his company Behance, joined Harvard Business School and got married all in the same year. He started several external relationships simultaneously, but it worked out well as his self-team had the agility, burstiness and cohesion to move back and forth between his person, professional and partner pods. The most important thing to understand here is that it is absolutely fine to not get an external fit for every P pod.

If you are not a boxer, you won't enter a boxing ring. You know that you neither have the competence nor any interest in boxing. Of course some areas in life are not as clear as a boxing ring. People enter those areas which do not fit them well out of conditioning, peer pressure or learned helplessness.

Though he lived in his own head most of the time, Albert Einstein had a wife and children. He could not handle the emotional demands made by his wife and drew a professional contract with her. His son, Eduard, struggled with mental illness while Hans, the other son, said, 'Probably the only project he ever gave up on was me.'[20]

When people understand their self-team better, they know when their partner pod or parent pod is not activated enough for an external fit and hence, they would not go for the same. Any individual, whose personal and professional pods are hyperactive, would be insanely focussed on himself and his ambitions. Such individuals, irrespective of gender and profession, choose to live a life focussed on personal accomplishments, without forging external bonds with their partner and parent pods. If your happiness lies in perfecting your passion, go ahead and do it without creating external fits that could become disastrous. Partner with your passion rather than a real person.

After three brief marriages, the American actor, comedian and author Whoopi Goldberg felt that she was the common denominator in all the failed marriages. 'I'm the round peg, and marriage is the square hole. You can't have a square hole, can you?' she says.[21] It took her some time to realize that not everyone is cut out for marriage.

An evolved and aligned self-team will help one to become more self-aware, well in time. People tend to rush into relationships because they are afraid of being alone, of being judged. Availability is a sad excuse to start a relationship. Relate with your self-team before rushing into or postponing an external connection.

---

[20]Ibid. 213–14.
[21]Vagianos, Alanna, 'Whoopi Goldberg on Marriage: "I Don't Want Somebody in My House"', *HuffPost*, 1 September 2016, https://bit.ly/39Nzxn5. Accessed on 4 May 2022.

Rachel Maddow is an American television news programme host and liberal political commentator. She came out as gay in the first year of her undergraduate degree at Stanford in 1990. She has been living with her partner Susan Mikula for the last 20 years. She builds her show in a unique manner where she admittedly feels like a 'news surgeon' who dissects information and fixes its interpretation so that it makes sense, all without getting emotional or angry about it. Her strong and self-aware self-team knows that she is not very good with people. 'Oh, I'm not a captain. I mean, if I was a parent, the children would starve, you know? Like, I can't really deal with hirings and firings and vacations and birthdays and keeping people happy. I'm blessed with producers who are really good with humans. I focus entirely on editorial content,' she admits.[22] This self-realization has kept her from adopting children.

A self-teamer has four P pods to begin. They are activated as the seeds inside begin to blossom. Some pods fully evolve, while some don't. It is fine either way. The important thing is to be aware of the competence of your self-team and second, to be willing to keep it aligned. Not turning into a partner, a professional or a parent is alright, turning into a half-hearted and half-baked one is not.

Dr A.P.J. Abdul Kalam invested in his professional side where he excelled as a scientist and the head of State. He invested in his personal piece and excelled as a creative, authentic thinker. He mentored his staff, students and readers

---

[22]Reitman, Janet, 'Rachel Maddow: The Rolling Stone Interview', *Rolling Stone*, 25 June 2018, https://bit.ly/3KJXBnk. Accessed on 4 May 2022.

and kindled the fire to excel. But, he did not look for an external life partner or biological children. It should be a norm not to have external fits for all the pods if an individual chooses to do so. Also, the fits can be replaced or renewed. Thus, a self-teamer will be called a **S**um of **P**erson, **P**rofessional, **P**artner, **P**arent and **P**erennial in **Y**ou to **C**reate **E**xcellence (aka SPYCE).

A self-teamer has the potential to be a SPYCE person, a SPYCE professional, a SPYCE partner, a SPYCE parent and a SPYCE perennial. First, they prepare the self-team and then connect with the right external fit, whose self-team is evolved and aligned too.

RAHUL DRAVID: THE WALL WITH ALL PS

'If you cannot get along with Dravid, you are struggling in life,' says one of his colleagues.

Known for his competence and conduct among his colleagues as well as his kin, Rahul Dravid is a wolf who lives for the pack.

Dravid has been consciously moving forward with all the chosen roles of a professional, a partner, a parent and, of course, a person. As a person, his focussed hard work and humility have been his constant companions. He started playing professional cricket at the young age of 12, pursuing his passion for close to three decades. His records in International test cricket are an integral part of cricket lore, while his one day innings show the kind of discipline and deep practice he brought to the table. Though he is a fierce combination of professional success, fame and riches,

Dravid is unequivocally known as 'Mr Dependable'. His life partner, Vijeta, asserts that he never brought his celebrity 'crown' home. Away from the limelight, he enjoys being a doting husband and an immersive dad. He transitions into his 'personal' roles in the domestic realm with the fluidity of an artist and proceeds to play the 'coach' role in the professional realm with an assured agility.

Dravid is surely a sum of person, professional, partner, parent and perennial who has created excellence in each role. He is a 'SPYCE' guy. He plays all the innings of his life with agility and alertness. While a cool and composed captain, he never forgot to be a consistent batsman nor underplayed being a dependable husband. At the time of writing this book, he was busy infusing excellence into the U-19 cricket team as a coach, without compromising on his parent role. Dravid politely declined an honorary doctorate degree which was conferred on him by Bangalore University asserting that he would want to earn it someday.

Dravid chose to become a coach for the young Indian team when other lucrative offers were open to him because he wished to pay it forward. His exemplary conduct shines through. A celebrity who effortlessly stands in a queue with his children, a coach who encourages every cricketing U-19 team, Dravid is a rare gem. Everyone, from his teammates to his opponents, look up to him for his humility, someone who is open to criticism. He is someone who has strengthened his internal self-team of four P pods: person, professional, partner and parent. He is someone who values himself in all these roles. He has mastered the craft of moving with agility between different P roles while mindfully choosing an external fit for every internal member. Hence, he is an agile role shifter and an alert internal–external fitter.

SELF-TEAMING NUGGETS

- Say 'goodbye' to perfection in one domain. Be 'good enough' in all.
- Acknowledge all the Ps: person, professional, partner and parent—your self-team of small giants.
- Make your children acknowledge their Ps at the earliest. Encourage them to be rounded individuals.
- Engage in self-talk in solitude to help yourself catalyse different pods by becoming more self-aware.
- Recalibrate your self-team with each new pod being catalysed. Let the pods have a good time with each other.
- Let agility, burstiness and cohesion grow between different pods of your self-team so that respect and trust develop.
- Create proper internal alignment between P pods before looking for and working for an external fit.
- Remember, it is totally fine to not get an external fit for every P pod. Had Einstein known his self-team, his wife and children would have been spared.
- Cultivate social courage to nurture your self-team.

AND GAMING

THE COUPLE THAT SHATTERS STEREOTYPES EVERY DAY

At nine, she would plough the fields and pull out leeches from the wet rice fields, alongside her father who always welcomed the much-needed help. At 18, she won the first National Women's Boxing Championship. At 22, she married Onler Kom, a law student from the same community. He ferociously believed in her talent as a boxer and pushed her to do better professionally.

At 24, she became a mother to twin boys, winning two world boxing championships and the Padma Shri in 2006. At 36, she had her third child. An active boxer, Mary Kom, also known as Magnificent Mary, is the only woman to have won a medal in each of the seven world boxing championships and a Padma Bhushan.

Mary Kom and Onler Kom is a couple defying gender stereotypes, cultural conditioning and conventional wisdom. And guess what, their coupledom works. Kangathei, the village in Manipur where Mary Kom belongs, is a small, orthodox place where her parents lived as landless farmers who lived by hunting, fishing, farming, wood-cutting or other menial jobs. Despite their penury, they sent their children to school, barely managing to pay the fees.

Strenuous physical work was an integral part of their lives and Mary helped in the fields as well as in the kitchen. Her physical stamina grew as she raced to school, tended to the cattle, ploughed the fields, and plucked fruits and vegetables. Her father never shied away from acknowledging her interest in sports. She won almost all competitions in middle school. She was admitted to a school in the capital city of Imphal to pursue sports. During the ninth and tenth grades, she stayed with different relatives, trying to get a hang of sports like athletics, gymnastics and javelin throw, but nothing excited her. Without telling her parents, she dabbled in a sport that was at the time considered a man's domain—boxing. When she won a gold medal at the first major tournament, her father reluctantly agreed to her getting into professional boxing. They saved each and every penny to help Mary continue her training at different government-run associations and private academies.

Onler was the president of the Komrem Students' Union (KRSU) in Delhi, where he was studying law. He met young Mary in 2000 at a training camp in Delhi. He checked on her as a well-wisher. While travelling for an important selection camp to Hisar in 2001, Mary lost her passport in the train along with her suitcase. She got selected for the international championship and urgently needed a new passport. Onler not only ran from pillar to post in Delhi get a new passport issued, he in fact travelled to Hisar to deliver the passport to her.[23]

In December 2001, she was selected to participate in the World Women's Boxing Championship being held in Pennsylvania, US. Her father could manage only ₹2,000 for the trip. She shared her problem with Onler, who organized a meeting of friends and elders of the Kom community in Delhi to find ways to raise the needed funding. President of the Union, Manipur, was present in the meeting who suggested that the boys meet the two Members of Parliament from Manipur and ask for help. Onler did so and the two MPs contributed ₹5,000 and ₹3,000. Thus, Onler became a part of Mary's struggle, a problem-solver and a motivator.

Mary had no friends, only colleagues. She only spoke Manipuri. Hence, Onler, who spoke her language, became her emotional anchor. They were honest to each other. Onler confided in her about his recent break-up after a long relationship. Observing Mary's unwavering commitment to her sport, Onler always motivated her to stay focussed and frugal.

Her boxing achievements won her the Arjuna Award in 2003 and marriage proposals started pouring in. Onler was scared for two reasons. He feared that her father might agree

---

[23]Kom, Mary and Dina Serto, *Meri Kahani: M.C. Mary Kom Unbreakable*, Manjul Publishing House, 2014.

with some unsuitable match who would scuttle her career. He also dreaded the scenario where Mary, being naïve, might fall for some insecure guy. Onler understood Mary's fears and her passion for boxing, her determination to compete. So, he proposed to her. 'I want to marry you to protect your career,' he said.

He gave up his job in the customs and excise department to be with Mary. From the very beginning, he knew that theirs would be an unusual partnership, in which the kitchen was Onler's domain, while Mary pursued her career as a boxer and a sub-inspector. However, Onler managed all the domestic duties well while Mary won laurels for the country. She became a mother to twins in August 2007. Throughout her pregnancy and after childbirth, the people and the press suspected the end of Mary's career. Even her father advised her to hang up her gloves, but Onler and Mary knew what she was made of.

She took care of the babies for a year. Nursing two of them throughout the day and night was exhausting. Onler took all the night duties upon himself, making it a real equal partnership. He showed that a man can excel in the domestic domain with ease.

In the last two decades, Mary has been a medal winner in all the international women's boxing championships. She has won an Olympic medal and a Commonwealth Games medal and is still going strong. Onler has actively raised their three sons, bonded with the whole family and ran the Mary Kom Boxing Academy while Mary Kom trained, travelled and made everyone proud.

People like Onler prove that life should not be segregated

into gender domains, but rather lived with a fluid mindset. It should not be played like an 'or' game between 'women in kitchens' and 'men in offices'. It should be an 'and' game, where gender-specific separatism doesn't exist.

Not all men wish to wear the mask of masculinity that symbolizes power and control. Not all women wish to revel in feminine fineries that symbolize softness and submission. 'And Gaming' offers solutions to both men and women to become free from stereotypes and restrictions.

WHAT IS AND GAMING?

And Gaming is the antitheses to the 'separate spheres' ideology based on patriarchal division of society.

The separate sphere ideology divides the domain of the alpha male and the beta female in such a way that the former should occupy the public sphere, the workplace, while the latter should avoid it, restricting themselves to the domestic domain.

This social ideology has mandated for centuries that a man should stimulate the personal and the professional pods of his self-team, while a woman should stimulate the partnerial and the parental pods of her self-team.

As per the separate spheres ideology, men should focus on their roles as a person and as a professional, while a woman should focus on her roles as a partner and a parent. And Gaming refutes this separation. It expects man and woman both to embrace all their roles with neutrality and excellence.

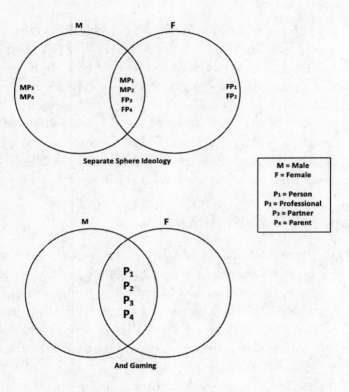

The gender-based division of labour worked in the Industrial Age, which divided the working spheres of men and women. During that age, the idea of marriage was equated to that of a factory, says Justin Wolfers, an economist at University of Michigan.[24] A factory succeeds on the degree of specialization. In a marriage, the man was specialized

---

[24]'The age of hedonic marriage', *The Economist*, 18 January 2008, https://econ.st/3wOvcYH. Accessed on 16 May 2022.

to work in the market, while the woman would work at home. The woman was given the complex, but mundane and non-paying job of running the household. Men gave her the power to run the home since they did not want this power. So, they declared that women were better at it. Thus, marriage remained productive when women worked at home and men worked outside.

In this intelligence-infused information age, neither is marriage based on the idea of a factory, nor are men and women productive complementarities. Times have changed. Running the household is less complex and less physically demanding. Women have equal access to education, information and entertainment. Hence, each one of us wants to learn and earn, experience and experiment, and wishes to taste power and pleasure.

The dynamics of families is changing. Today, the way leaders decide to take their countries forward, the way partners decide to raise their families has a new narrative. The prime minister of a developed nation like Canada talks about equality, empathy, globalism and forgiveness as his philosophy. He apologizes with aplomb. He cries and puts his vulnerability out there. Players like Serena Williams essay their roles of a tennis player and a parent like a symphony. Indian boxer Mary Kom continues to compete, with her three children being an integral part of her daily vision of life. Satya Nadella runs Microsoft with the energy of empathy fuelling the core businesses. He admits that the father in him has shaped the leader in him.

The walls between the masculine and feminine roles are gradually breaking, giving way to an 'and' game. We need to put our cultural 'learned helplessness' behind us and embrace a more inclusive viewpoint. Our cultural trappings have built stereotypes which need to be toppled over and new bridges be built. No man is happy and content by merely being a poster boy of power. No woman feels fulfilled by merely being a domestic custodian. The only way to achieve 360 degree excellence is by being an 'and gamer'.

HOW TO BE AN 'AND GAMER'

An 'And Gamer' is an excellence enthusiast who is equally ready to fly a plane and to raise a family, who is equally enthusiastic to negotiate strategically at work and also to whip a meal at home. Here is how you can become an 'and gamer'.

Redefine the Partnership Called 'Marriage': A marriage today is as essential for us as a chauffeur to drive our car. If one loves driving, they don't need a chauffeur. If one loves travelling but is not stuck on the idea of owning a car, they neither need a car nor a chauffeur. If one is ready to experiment with other modes of transport, a chauffeur is not needed. However, if one loves the idea of having someone to drive them around, being chivalrous enough to hold the door open for them or having the car ready at the doorstep and enjoying a nap in the back seat, a chauffeur is a must.

To many, Wi-Fi has taken precedence over marriage. It might become 'the Kodak debacle' of this century unless it manages a makeover. The institution of marriage has undergone much change in the last few decades. These changes are at three levels: economic, emotional and erotic. As both men and women become financially autonomous, marriage needs to be redesigned on an economic level.

As meanings of infidelity and trust are fading in a virtual world, as partners sit alone on marital rubble while posting happy pictures online, marriage needs to be redefined on an emotional level. As the history of marriage states that it was always an economic enterprise whose primary motive was stability, not love, marriage needs to be inclusive on an erotic level.[25] Unless marriage is redefined on these three levels, the tribe of 'and gamers' will not rise and the institution of marriage will decline globally.

Finland, a small European country, has the world's best school system. Also, it had a very high divorce rate—close to 60 per cent, in 2019.[26] Despite having an egalitarian education system, families are crumbling. Men and women, who are learning to be equal, open, creative and trustworthy since childhood are failing to connect with the existing model of marriage. A noteworthy reality is that Finnish women consider divorce far more than Finnish men. It simply means that equality taught in schools doesn't get translated into marriages, which are trapped in traditions of yore.

When Denmark was the world's second-happiest country (after Finland) in 2020, the divorce rate that year was 48 per cent.[27] It means that happiness caused by equality

[25]Cohn, Gretta, 'Why Marry? (Part 1) (Ep. 155)', Freakonomics, freakonomics.com/podcast/why-marry-part-1-a-new-freakonomics-radio-podcast/.

[26]'Divorce rates in Europe in 2019, by country', *Statista*, https://bit.ly/3MjBK85. Accessed on 16 May 2022.

[27]'Divorces', Statistics Denmark, https://bit.ly/3ljUbxj. Accessed on 16 May 2022.

and freedom in countries like Finland and Denmark more than compensate for the grief caused by divorces.

In countries like India where 'cornerstone' model of marriage was considered the eternal truth of adulthood, the social dynamics are churning. Intelligent, financially independent, skilled and mature men and women are gaping at the 'capstone' model, which enables them to marry late, more for emotional stability and equality than for social box-ticking.[28] So, a remodelled marriage on the three levels would need a fundamental shift.

1. **Economic Shift:** The 'partner' pod of the self-team needs to understand the importance of 'singleness' and 'jointness' in the economic piece of life. Anyone, husband or wife could be earning more. A stay-at-home dad should be as welcome as a stay-at-home mom. A mindset change is needed to bring about economic equilibrium in the marriage, for the spouse as well as for the children (if any). Address the monetary issues clearly, the way Nidhi did. A woman earning or a woman outearning her husband should not erode a man's ego, not any more. 'If your manhood is tied up in your wallet, there's a problem,' says actor Whoopi Goldberg.[29]

   Excellence is a choice that we make. It is a responsibility that we take for ourselves. Economic excellence in a marriage or partnership is achieved when all the partners have equal access to the family income. Less access to

---

[28]Cherlin, Andrew J., *The Marriage-Go-Round: The State of Marriage and the Family in America Today*, Vintage Books, 2010.

[29]Goldberg, Whoopi, *If Someone Says "You Complete Me," RUN!: Whoopi's Big Book of Relationships*, Hachette Books; First Edition, 2015.

the money earned by the family can trap one partner in a suboptimal life, eroding the quality of marriage.

Money is the road to self-reliance. Any adult who stops another adult from earning money by way of suggestion or correction is committing a crime. Any adult who gives in to it is complicit in the crime. Since most of the professional colleges in India have around 50 per cent girl's enrolment, girls are certainly studying to earn a degree which can be used to earn a living. Each adult, especially women should save enough in the first five to seven years of their career to take a break for parenting if needed. Let money be a part of your critical conversations if your day-to-day survival depends on someone, in case you take a break from earning.

Parents can certainly spend less on their children's wedding and instead contribute to a fund to keep the daughter self-reliant. Also, every marriage aspirant must know what it means legally to get married and they must meet a divorce lawyer to understand what causes marriages to fail. An economic understanding of worst-case scenarios is a must.

2. **Emotional Shift:** Katharine Meyer Graham, the noted American publisher of *The Washington Post,* talks about her marriage in her autobiography *Personal History.*[30] Her father Eugene Meyer owned the newspaper and made her husband Philip Graham the publisher after their marriage. Though Katharine, a student of the Madeira School and the University of Chicago, worked at a newspaper in San Francisco before getting married, her

---

[30]Graham, Katharine, *Personal History*, Alexandria Library, 2008.

father considered Phil and not her when it came to handling the business.

Similarly, Katharine described her marriage as a socially sanctioned script where she accepted her role as a kind of second-class citizen. 'As for Phil, at the same time, that he was building me up, he was tearing me down. As he emerged more on the journalistic and political scenes, I increasingly saw myself as the tail to his kite,' she writes.

In a marriage or any partnership, most males, by virtue of their upbringing, take a patriarchal stance. Katharine says further that Phil used his sharp wit and cruel humour on everyone, including her, making her the butt of family jokes. She felt that whenever she addressed any gathering, he would look at her in such a way as if to tell her that she was speaking for too long or boring everyone. The design of marriage needs to make this emotional shift where no partner attempts to dumb down the other.

Women are made to believe that they are inherently inferior to and psychologically dependent on men, that their problems are *their* fault. Candice Kumai, a known model and author in the US, is half Japanese and was teased and bullied in school for her looks. When she was young, she believed that she shouldn't be famous and successful because then she would not get a man. Our society wants us to believe that sought-after men do not want successful women for marriage.

Unless 'and gamers' make an emotional shift in a marriage by making it gender neutral and an integrated, not segregated, labour of love and respect, intimacy and independence, the institution of marriage will topple. Emotional fulfilment of each partner is the bedrock of a modern marriage.

3. **Erotic Shift:** Historically, marriage was rigid and mundane. It was accepted to be devoid of freedom for one partner and that was the norm. Love or eroticism was never the prime motive of marriage. It was based on boundaries of boredom. Fulfilment of the vagaries of one's heart happened on its fringes. The modern marriage seeks stability as well as adventure, love as well as limits. It needs to redefine the meaning of infidelity as well as faithfulness. To be an 'and gamer', one must recognize the importance of erotic blueprints of both the partners, i.e. a knowledge of what excites one's senses and how one is hardwired for pleasure. It is very important to communicate one's pathway to pleasure to the other partner for a long-lasting relationship.

Instant connectivity with friends and strangers leads to a quick expression of intimacy. Deficit of attention and patience leads to a constant search for something exciting. Relationship expert Esther Perel suggests having multiple marriages with the same person to keep the marriage rejuvenated.

Marriage is becoming a tough road to travel in this digital world. The road to revelry can turn into a road to rivalry as soon as a trail of messages is found in the partner's phone. Interpretation of fidelity and infidelity has never been more fluid. Is sexual exclusivity equal to faithfulness while you are emotionally attached to someone else? Is emotional loyalty equal to fidelity while you sext for fun? Is micro cheating (digital infidelity) equal to unfaithfulness?

These new questions need new answers from our 'partner' pods. We need to make marriages sexually authentic or else, short-term dalliances will become the norm. Marriage is a social mandate in our culture, an essential route to social nirvana. But millennials have started questioning the purpose of a rigid, farcical marriage. Hence, an economic, emotional and erotic refurbishing of marriage is warranted.

Change the Way We Raise Our Children: Women are far more active on online platforms than men except on Wikipedia. Women feel free to express themselves on platforms like Facebook and Twitter but Wikipedia makes them uncomfortable. The working culture of Wikipedia differs from other online communities. Wikipedia is the largest encyclopaedia in history where each editor is a self-appointed volunteer who can edit articles. Other volunteer editors can reverse the edits if they don't like it. If your article is considered irrelevant, it can be deleted. When an editor deletes someone's edits, he writes a mean message to that person.

John Riedl, a professor of computer science at University of Minnesota, studied Wikipedia.[31] The research showed that only 16 per cent of the new editors joining Wikipedia in 2009 identified themselves as female, and those females made only

---

[31]University of Minnesota, 'University of Minnesota researchers reveal Wikipedia gender biases', https://bit.ly/3LKaUES. Accessed on 5 May 2022.

9 per cent of the edits by the editors who joined that year. He observed that men delete most of the articles written by women. Women edit less because they feel they have less time. Their edits get deleted more. Also, women do not like to invite unnecessary conflict and rejection.

Thus, the study concluded that women react differently to conflict and competition. When I read this story, I wanted to find the reason behind this difference in behaviour between the two sexes. We have been told that men are from Mars and women are from Venus. But are we born or raised that way?[32]

Uri Gneezy and John A. List answered this question through their life experiments conducted in Africa and India.[33] They visited a patriarchal Masai village in Tanzania where a man, when asked how many children he had, would only take into account the number of boys. Then, they visited a matrilineal Khasi village in Meghalaya, India, where children take their mother's family name, the youngest daughter inherits the family inheritance, and the men cannot buy property and move into their wives' house (or live with their sisters if they don't marry).

In both the places, they played a small game with the men and the women. Each person was given 10 chances to toss a tennis ball underhand into a bucket kept 10 feet away. Each person was matched with an unidentified person and given two options. First, they could win one dollar

[32]Lechtenberg, Suzie, 'Women Are Not Men' (Ep. 116), Freakonomics, https://bit.ly/3chmUSH. Accessed on 5 May 2022.
[33]Gneezy, Uri and John A. List, *The Why Axis: Hidden Motives and the Undiscovered Economics of Everday Life*, Random House Business Books, 2013.

for every ball landing in the bucket or get three dollars for each ball landing in the bucket if they managed to put more balls in the bucket than the unidentified competitor. In the patriarchal Masai village, 50 per cent of the Masai men chose the competitive option, while 54 per cent of the Khasi women chose the competitive option.

This research showed that if girls are raised in an environment where making decisions, dealing with money and delegating work is a part of their lives, they will be just as competitive as men.

Thus, for 'and gaming', we need to raise our children differently. Let us learn about the key behavioural shifts needed for the same.

Spare Children from Conventional Gender Stereotypes: The catalogue from the biggest chain of toy shops in Denmark, BR, shows boys playing with Barbie dolls and girls playing with trains. That girls should eat less and laugh less and boys can't cry are such stereotypes ingrained in our collective psyche. Boys and girls should neither be exposed to colour-coded clothing nor to behavioural masking.

We prepare boys and girls for a suboptimal life when a girl in a math class is laughed at and a boy in a kitchen is bullied. These stereotypes mess up their natural orientation and talents before they can blossom. Let all the colours, all the toys, belong to all the children. Also, parents need to shun gender-based division of work because children mirror the behaviours of their parents. A submissive mother may perhaps signal a young daughter to bow down, while an aggressive father might signal a young son to boss around. When both parents integrate submission and aggression, sons and daughters will embrace both emotions with ease and real 'and gamers' will be born.

Apprise Children of Benevolent Sexism: Author Deepa Narayan interviewed Indian professional women working in metros for her book *Chup: Breaking the Silence About India's Women*.[34] During the course of writing the book, she studied the language/verbal cues and non-verbal cues/body language of these women. The subjects used words like 'nice', 'nurturing' and 'loving' to voice their positives and words like 'sacrificing', 'suffering' and 'not achieving the dreams' to voice their negatives.

Women use 'ladylike' body language which is not over-friendly or noisy, as is expected from them. Women succumb to these expectations and make the next generation succumb to that set of stereotypes too. When a girl is appreciated for doing mundane jobs at home or when she is made to feel pure but a weak person who needs to be protected by men, she must regard this attitude as benevolent sexism. When a boy is appreciated for being a protector or a provider, he must understand that as benevolent sexism.

Girls should be made aware of the general tendency that men have of giving women the power that they themselves don't want. They 'give' women the power to run the home, to deal with the children and to make domestic decisions, all of which can be collectively termed as a 'patronizing bait'.

Not only that—men tend to dilute the achievements of

[34]Narayan, Deepa, *Chup: Breaking the Silence about India's Women*, Juggernaut, 2018.

women, making them seem trivial and insignificant, while women tend to overemphasize the accomplishments of their male counterparts. Tina Brown, in her memoir *The Vanity Fair Diaries* mentions how her employers at *Tatler* magazine always made comparisons between her and her successor at *Tatler,* Libby Purves.[35] 'Libby did not have two of your most important attributes—your looks and your lifestyle,' opined the employers. Woman's accomplishments are benevolently reduced to their looks and appearance, something men never face.

Children should be taught not to fall for such sexist behaviours. If a husband says with pride that his wife doesn't earn because he earns enough money or a family addresses a mother who gives importance to her career as well as children as selfish, the next generation is in trouble. A well-raised child will know that every person must have a choice to excel in as many roles as they want.

Give Children a Peripatetic View of Life: When a person travels or works in various places for shorter periods, they develop what is called a 'peripatetic view'. Children, at a very young age, should be given a solid foundation, strong roots on which they can build their life and grow. They should know how to cook for themselves, how to earn, how to take care of someone, and most importantly, how to control and regulate their emotions, particularly anger and jealousy (which can be quite rampant given today's fierce competitiveness). The way children clean and cook in Japanese schools, the way

---

[35]Brown, Tina, *The Vanity Fair Diaries: 1983–1992*, Henry Holt and Co.; First Edition, 2017.

they learn money management in Peruvian schools are examples to emulate. These methods can go a long way in making them responsible citizens. It is necessary to expose our children to various roles that they might want to play in the future. They need to know that there is more to life than earning money and having a job. They should be raised to be rounded human beings. They should be motivated to cultivate competition as well as collaboration, performance as well as patience and competence as well as compassion to develop their self-team from an early age itself. Thus, in order to raise 'and gamers' of the future, we need to raise gender-agnostic families. We need to raise our boys better so that they do not become gender-biased.

Meher Pudumjee, chairperson of Thermax Ltd, recollects her childhood as a gender-agnostic one, where she and her brother Kurush were not subjected to any gender-specific conditioning. She was interested in the sciences and grew up to be an engineer, while her brother, who loved knitting and cooking, was welcome in the kitchen.[36]

We can't apply bandages to old wounds when we need corrective surgery. Great minds are androgynous. If we raise creative children, they have the strengths of not only their own gender but that of the other too. We need to raise psychologically androgynous children who are aggressive and nurturing, sensitive and rigid, dominant and submissive, irrespective of gender.

---

[36]'238: 22.01 Meher Pudumjee: Early Formative Years from Play to Potential Podcast', Stitcher, https://bit.ly/3KJ9CcP. Accessed on 5 May 2022.

Learn the Strategies to Balance the Power between Genders: Statistics released by the United Nations Office on Drugs and Crime (UNODC) in 2017 reveal that more than half the women murdered worldwide were killed by their intimate partners or family members.[37] This research indicates an imbalance of power play between women and men. The American education system consisted of segregated schools for the African-American and white population for a very long time. These schools were theoretically based on 'separate, but equal' ideology. The schools for the African-American never got the same kind of infrastructural or financial support as the white schools, but they were expected to feel grateful for whatever they got.[38]

I hear the same sentiment echoed in our social corridors where boys and girls are treated 'separate, but equal' and girls are expected to be happy with slivers of freedom that they are given.

In the city of Topeka, Kansas, Oliver and Leola Brown lived with their seven-year-old daughter Linda, who studied in a black school, Munroe. Since the school was far from their house, Leola wished to enrol her daughter in a white school, Summer. When the principal refused to admit an African-American to a white school, the Black civil rights body sued the Topeka Board of Education.

The famous *Brown v. Board of Education* became a

---

[37]UNODC, 'The Women Killed on One Day around the World', BBC News, 25 November 2018, www.bbc.com/news/world-46292919. Accessed on 5 May 2022.
[38]'Separate but Equal: The Law of the Land', https://s.si.edu/3wtaVaI. Accessed on 6 May 2022.

landmark case in the history of American education as it ruled the practice of segregation as unconstitutional.

However, author and podcast presenter Malcolm Gladwell points out that there was a huge difference between what the Black community aspired for and what the court dictated.[39]

What the African-American community aspired for was power, what was handed to them was pity. We hear the same sentiment echoing between men and women. What women desire and deserve is power, what men dole out is patronizing behaviour. Similarly, when men desire and deserve understanding, what women dole out is judgement. Let's look at the ways to strategize power balance between man and woman.

Create Happiness for Both: Economists Betsy Stevenson and Justin Wolfers conducted a study on female happiness which revealed that 50 years ago, females were far happier with their lives, while men reported greater life satisfaction now.[40] This 'happiness paradox' shows that with greater autonomy, more power, financial independence and added social responsibility, women are growing increasingly unhappy. This is so because they then need to work harder, taking some of the economic load off men, but men still don't share much of the domestic load. While women have gone out of their homes to study and work, men have not gone

---

[39]Maine, Emily, 'The Foot Soldier of Birmingham with Malcolm Gladwell: Revisionist History Podcast Transcript,' Medium, 7 July 2017, https://bit.ly/3yg74Av. Accessed on 5 May 2022.

[40]Stevenson, Betsey and Justin Wolfers, 'The Paradox of Declining Female Happiness', *American Economic Journal: Economic Policy*, American Economic Association, August 2009, 1(2): 190–225.

inside the homes to raise the kids and do the laundry.

So, the partner pod of our self-team should be prepared to perform the mundane jobs as well as the 'magical' ones. Each one of us should be readied to make the bed as well as make money.

Also, now that women have taken up important roles in the professional sphere, they have come to realize that they are underpaid in comparison to their male counterparts and undervalued for their domestic contributions. They are more disillusioned as they can see the possibilities out there and how they feel restricted doing unproductive and unacknowledged work in the office and at home.

So, we have two strategies to reduce this unhappiness and disillusionment. First, to share the humdrum load with their partner. Share the prosaic equally to share the phenomenal and thus each one of us performs a mix of ordinary and extraordinary tasks. Research proves that Scandinavian men are more involved in childcare as well as domestic work than their British counterparts.[41] Research from University of Missouri shows that men and women are happier when they share household chores and child-rearing responsibilities.[42] Second, acknowledge and appraise the contributions of the domestic domain. The partnering and parenting competence should be computed and given its rightful place on a person's résumé.

---

[41]Altintas, Evrim and Oriel Sullivan, 'Trends in Fathers' Contribution to Housework and Childcare under Different Welfare Policy Regimes', *Social Politics: International Studies in Gender, State & Society*, 2017, 24(1): 81–108.
[42]'The secret to a happy marriage appears to be housework', Today, 15 June 2013, https://on.today.com/3LIbuDY. Accessed on 5 May 2022.

State and Organizational Support: The district growth curves of East and West Germany during the four decades, from 1949 to 1989, manifest how national culture can impact the lives of men and women. After the Second World War, communist East Germany lost big businesses like Siemens and Allianz to capitalist West Germany. Owing to more chances of economic growth in West Germany, men moved towards West Germany. East Germany needed women to work in all areas, from moving cranes to running hospitals. So, they welcomed women to work and study science as well as religion, while the women in West Germany needed their husband's permission to work till 1977.[43]

In these 40 years, East Germany opened free childcare centres, offered parent money, i.e. a generously paid 14-month parental leave, out of which a father needs to compulsorily take two months leave. In Western Germany, women earned 21 per cent less than their male counterparts, while in Eastern Germany, they earned only 8 per cent lesser. In Western Germany, a mother leaving her child in day care is considered a 'bad mother', while in Eastern Germany, nine out 10 women work outside home.[44] Supportive childcare infrastructure and the availability of jobs and education for women have created a gender-neutral culture in East Germany which has enabled women to excel in all realms of life.

While American and British citizens strive for more

---

[43]*The Policy on Gender Equality in Germany*, Directorate-General of Internal Policies, 2015, https://bit.ly/384cofu. Accessed on 5 May 2022.

[44]Hamilton, Valeria, 'Women in Germany's East Earn Close to What Men Do. Can We Thank Socialism for That?', The World, https://bit.ly/3KQ4Z0C. Accessed on 5 May 2022.

money, Scandinavians strive for more time. Instead of labouring around the clock and then outsourcing the domestic work, Danes would use their time doing jobs like cleaning, cooking and gardening. Subsidized childcare and less working hours enable 78 per cent of Danish mothers to return to work after having children.[45]

To become 'and gamers', a two-pronged strategy for change is needed at two levels. First, need-based changes in government policies and industry support for an improved gender dynamic at work and at home. Second, a change in mindset.

In Germany, businesses like Siemens have started day care centres near production sites. It organizes a high school science camp for bright female maths and physics students and mentors female undergraduates. Starting crèches is just the beginning. A social re-engineering model needs to be in place where organizations have physical spaces for older children to sit, study, read, nap or play indoor games.

Companies like ICICI Bank, Nestlé and Godrej Consumer Products Ltd offer travel accompaniment policies for children and nannies when senior female executives travel. Along with the policy shift, we need to create a cultural shift, where nothing is gender specific apart from giving birth. Financial autonomy for each man and woman needs to be ensured by putting practical strategies in place. We haven't got them in place because the powerful enjoy the status quo and the powerless can't push the envelope enough.

Matrimony or parenthood should not make a woman hand over her day-to-day survival to others. A 'self-reliance

---

[45]Russell, Helen, *The Year of Living Danishly: Uncovering the Secrets of the World's Happiest Country*, Icon Books Ltd; Reissue edition, 2015, p. 143.

fund' should be propagated by every employer for whosoever wishes to take a maternity/paternity leave. The best way to predict the future is to create it.

The Use of Technology to Create Balance of Power: A real 'and game' is possible only when a household is considered a production hub, not merely a consumption hub. A homemaker or a house husband cooks hot meals, cleans the house, and provides childcare and/or eldercare, but economics doesn't consider it as 'production'. All the production in the domestic domain is considered as 'consumption'. This treatment needs modification.

In her book *More Work for Mother: The Ironies of Household Technology from the Open Hearth to the Microwave*, Professor Ruth Schwartz Cowan says that work has two components: time and metabolic labour.[46] Technology has reduced the latter, not the former. Also, where are we using the time freed by the technology developments? With more efficient washing machines, are we washing more linen or using the saved-up time to improve our productivity? With more efficient automobiles, are mothers busier taking children to various classes and doctors' appointments, or using the time for excelling in some other role? A radical change in our mindset is needed to take the benefit of technological advancements which could free up time from any domain to be used in other domains. It should not be consumed in creating unproductive frills in the same domain. If

[46]Cowan, Ruth Schwartz, *More Work for Mother: The Ironies of Household Technology from the Open Hearth to the Microwave,* Basic Books; Reprint edition, 1985.

automation can allow an executive to work from anywhere around some tasks, staying glued in office till late as a habit needs to be done away with.

Create New Job Profile of a Transition Coach: When bestselling author, journalist and speaker Helen Russell moved from London to a small town close to Copenhagen in Denmark, she came across the website of a cultural integration coach, Pernille Chaggar. She helped Helen understand how Danish life differed from a British life and how to adapt to Danish ways for a happy stay.

Workplaces need to have such transition coaches. It is the dawn of a new job, a new career—experts who mentor the 'parents to be' while they transition from their professional role into a parental role. If you are a PROTIP (Professional turning into Parent), you will need the services of a transition coach. They would aggregate data of all PROTIPs, and shadow their journey into parenthood and back into the workplace. They would become the bridge between a PROTIP and their workplace, current and potential.

Such coaches could design (craft) jobs for PROTIPs, to assimilate them gradually into the workforce after the parenting break.

Since they will have data of various PROTIPs, they could create a network of people and companies who could use their services. They would help young women to mentally prepare for life changes and mentor them to stay updated and upbeat to keep excelling in all P pods. A PROTIP would receive nurturing as well as nudging from a transition coach who would motivate them to enjoy parenthood while nudging them to stay professionally relevant. A transition coach will build a shared context between the professional and the parental pods of the self-team of a person. This shared context will be revised each year to prepare an updated résumé of the PROTIP when they decide to join the workforce back.

Prof. Herminia Ibarra of the London Business School, an authority on career transitions, says that since we attach much of our identity to our work, transitions can disorient a person.[47] When you are married to your work, transition might feel like a divorce. Hence, a transition coach is much-needed. Thus, to be an 'and gamer', we need a shift in the way we understand marriage and the way we raise our children. It also needs us to create new 'balance of power' strategies and the new job profile of a 'transition coach'.

INDRA AND RAJ NOOYI: WE CHOSE THE RIGHT PARTNERS

Though this role model famously declared, 'Woman can't have it all', she is one of those who have come real close to having it all. An Indian immigrant postgraduate student at Yale University, a management Consultant, the CEO of a conglomerate with market capital of $240.20 billion as of May 2022, married for 38 years, a mother of two children, Indra Nooyi believes in taking care of her extended family and giving it forward. Though she was not born in a gender-neutral family, her mother gave her the freedom to express herself

---

[47]'501: 47.04 Herminia Ibarra—Pausing to reinvent', Podcast 9, https://bit.ly/3Mkwsce. Accessed on 16 May 2022.

and opt for higher studies. She excelled in all the roles that she chose. Yet, the Indian mindset of women being domestic champions first, has echoed throughout her life. Indra says emphatically that she chose the right life partner Raj, who was from a similar background and had similar ideologies. Indra says that they survived because she never brought her corporate status home and Raj was an understanding man.

Her mother would make up improvised games that encouraged young Indra to speak up and take up different roles of imitating world leaders. Indra planned and prepared extensively to be a 'good enough' spouse and mother. She is known for getting up at four every morning and preparing breakfast for the family. Her secretary had clear-cut instructions to speak to her children about guiding them for various scenarios when they called their busy mother at work.

She couldn't attend all the school basketball games of her daughter but made sure that her children were proud of her. As a partner, she has adapted well. As a parent, she has been there for her children, with the support of her parents and extended family. As a professional, she has turned around a snack and cola company into a nutrition company. She has created products and movements by thinking like a woman and a parent. She has consolidated the culture of PepsiCo by being energetic and empathetic towards everything and everyone. As a person, she takes interest in reading and playing tennis. She has chosen to create excellence in all the roles that she has played.

Indra has always spoken about the need for gender parity. She candidly shared how she was expected to do the domestic odd jobs even when her brother or husband was around. From these experiences, it can be assumed that she must have raised her daughters in a gender-agnostic environment. She and her husband, who have had a great life partnership together, must have exemplified to their daughters the importance of androgyny and the value of creating a shared context.

When Nooyi opined that women can't have it all, it referred to the 'perfection' syndrome that women are expected to achieve. She admits that becoming a supermom and an 'ever-present' wife is not possible with a CEO position but being 'good enough' and 'striving for more than good enough' is certainly possible.

Raj and Indra Nooyi have been 'and gamers' throughout their lives as they debunked the separate spheres ideology and filled in for each other in different domains.

AND GAMING NUGGETS

- Remodel 'marriage' on an economic level by having critical conversations beforehand around money. Both partners should be ready to make the bed as well as money.
- Redefine 'marriage' on an emotional level by removing any matriarchal or patriarchal tilt and making it an integrated, not segregated, labour of love and respect, intimacy and independence for both partners.
- Redesign 'marriage' on an erotic level by clearly communicating one's erotic blueprint to the other and by enhancing sexual authenticity.
- Raise yourself before raising your children by renouncing

gender stereotypes like colour-coded stuff or behavioural masking (e.g. laughing at a boy in the kitchen or a girl in coding class).

- Teach yourself and your children to spot benevolent sexism.
- Be androgynous and raise androgynous children whose thoughts, actions and behaviour are gender neutral.
- Campaign for 'transition coaches' to enable you when you become a professional turning into parent (PROTIP).
- Campaign for and support policy changes by government and industries to improve gender dynamics at work and at home.

P PEDESTALLING

THE MAN WHO IS EQUAL PARTS HUSBAND, DAD, CEO AND HIMSELF

It was 1 February 2014. I was headed to Harvard Kennedy School, Boston, to attend an executive education programme on 'Leadership for the Twenty-First Century'. We were advised to think in advance about an adaptive leadership challenge that needed a solution.

At that time, I was writing a book on parenting titled *Don't Raise Your Children, Raise Yourself* and I tried to apply my learnings to the leadership challenge. I asked myself:

a) Is there a connection between parenting and leadership?

b) Can some transfer learning happen between the two?

To get answers to these questions, I circulated a small questionnaire among 65 course mates from 19 countries. Seventy-three per cent of them agreed to a strong connection between parenting and leadership. Many of them drew attention to how becoming a parent raised their game as a leader. A father to two young children swore by his patience, which had grown manifold after becoming a father. The director of a US hospital agreed that she learnt from her parenting experience to 'bow down to another's level'. Just like we try to get into a toddler's shoes to understand their perspective, we should do that to understand our juniors at work too. There were others who shared that they applied their time discipline and negotiating skills at home. My group members appreciated the idea and I started thinking about creating a course around it. It was in the same week, that a technocrat, originally from India, was named the CEO of Microsoft, the tech giant.

Satya Nadella called himself the 'unlikely CEO' of Microsoft, when the company was facing stiff competition from the likes of Apple, Google and Amazon, and needed transformation. Nadella was given the responsibility of heading MS as its third CEO in 40 years, only after Bill Gates and Steve Ballmer.[48]

Being at Harvard, learning about leadership from the best teachers, connecting it with my adaptive challenge and getting support for my thoughts made me generally optimistic. The appointment of Nadella added to this

---

[48]Nadella, Satya, *Hit Refresh: The Quest to Rediscover Microsoft's Soul and Imagine a Better Future for Everyone*, Chapter 1, HarperBusiness, 2019.

optimism. I have followed his journey ever since.

Nadella grew up in India in an unusual household. I call it unusual because it had working parents: an IAS father and an educationist (professor) mother. Yet, he was not forced to study and make it to the crème de la crème of Indian institutions—which was and still is, to some extent, a mandatory life goal for ambitious parents. What makes him truly unique is his realization as well as an honest acknowledgement of how his partner and parent pods have shaped him as a leader and an individual.

Nadella, as a 'consummate insider' at Microsoft, strived to change the culture at the organization by aligning the 'personal persona' (life persona) of the employees with their 'work persona'. He, from the very beginning, in 2014, has been trying to connect the 'home lives' and 'work lives' of people because he wants them to create products and services which are not 'needed' by its consumers but 'loved'. They have a Senior Leadership Team (SLT), which comprises some of the most talented engineers, researchers, managers and marketers at Microsoft. This team periodically meets to brainstorm, discuss and review big opportunities and solve problems. He has changed the context of these meetings by merging the personal and the professional. He tells his teammates, 'If we can connect what we stand for as individuals with what this company is capable of, there is very little we can't accomplish.'[49]

He says, 'My passion is to put empathy at the centre of everything I pursue—from the products we launch, to

---

[49]Ibid, Chapter 2.

the new markets we enter, to the employees, customers and partners we work with.' He has learnt and imbibed this empathy from being a father to his differently abled son Zain, who was born with cerebral palsy and to one of his daughter's (Divya), born with a learning disorder. In other words, he has put his parental perspective on a pedestal alongside his professional one.

He admits that his wife Anupama nudged him to feel empathy and not self-pity or resentment. Nadella keeps reminding himself of the influence his parents had on him— his father fired-up his intellectual curiosity, while his mother let him be.

It is not very easy to find a man who remembers and then reflects upon the struggles and dilemmas of his young mother. However, Nadella is one such man who remembers the pressure and the guilt of his mother, who wanted to balance her marriage with her career in the 1960s and '70s. He has put the learnings as a son on the CEO pedestal to give the right advice to women employees. In 2014, he suggested women not to ask for a raise but have faith in the company to give it. In 2018, during the course of writing his book, when he recalled his mother's experiences of balancing work and home, he realized his mistake. He suggested women advocate for themselves and took it upon leaders, like himself, to listen to what they were advocating. Amid his demanding career, he has maintained his passions: cricket and computers. He has been a learner who is ready to share while he is learning. He has responded to 'life and its lessons' in real time by writing *Hit Refresh* not in retrospect mode but in 'into' mode. He often brings his husband and father roles to meet his engineer-leader-mentor role at work.

As a professional, Nadella learnt electrical and industrial engineering to develop his passion for computing. He is a quick and agile learner who learnt computer sales, online search advertising, cloud computing and machine learning while building various businesses on the job. He fondly remembers his boss Doug Burgum, who thought about business and work not in isolation but as part of the societal fabric and a core part of one's life.[50] Nadella's leadership style is a set of principles based on the alchemy of purpose, innovation and empathy. He strongly believes in making choices as a leader.

He has been a steady and sturdy partner to his wife. They knew each other from school and took a liking for each other as they shared similar family values and were family friends. He loved his job at Microsoft, but he equally valued his love for Anu. They got married in 1992, while Anu was completing her architecture course and she applied for a US Visa in 1993. It got rejected because Nadella was a permanent resident. The immigration lawyer at Microsoft told him that it might take five or more years for Anu to come to the US. He gave up his permanent residency and took H1B visa as it enables the spouse of the applicant to come to the US. Even today, if you google, 'He surrendered green card and took H1B visa', the only name that comes up is that of Satya Nadella. Satya and Anu have been a permanent team through thick and thin as their relationship has gone from

---

[50]Kacka, Katarina, et al. 'Daymond John: The Power of Broke to Build Your Business', Lewis Howes, 20 January 2016, lewishowes.com/podcast/daymond-john/. Accessed on 5 May 2022.

strength to strength while raising three children.

Nadella recalls honestly that he was pondering about 'Why did it happen to us, to me?' when Anu made him realize that it is not about him, it was about Zain. Their partnership and constant communication of a shared context have shaped an empathetic Nadella for his family and for Microsoft.

He said, 'My son's condition requires that I draw daily upon the very same passion for ideas and empathy that I learned from my parents. And I do this both at home and at work.' He turned into an empathetic father which made empathy a core of his perspective. Parenthood occupies an active seat in his mind permanently because he keeps thinking, as a father as well as a technocrat, to use AI and other technologies to make life easy for children like Zain and Divya. Though Zain passed away in February 2022, his disability made his father empathetic enough to alter the vision statement of Microsoft which said, 'I define my mission and that of my company as empowering every person and every organization on the planet to achieve more.'

When their daughter was diagnosed with a learning disability, to the extent that none of the local schools could help her, the Nadellas found an academy in Vancouver. Anu shuttled their daughter to and from Canada for five years until she helped establish the academy's second branch in Washington. All this while Satya was leading Microsoft through a drastic transition and taking care of Zain in Seattle.

WHAT IS P PEDESTALLING?

Unlike some people who choose a multidimensional life to live, most of us are prepared to live a unidimensional life. Men chasing fulfilment in professional domain and women seeking fulfilment in domestic domain is the suboptimal life script offered by our culture. Excellence 360 degree is an attempt to challenge this suboptimal life script.

Life is not primarily a quest for pleasure, as Sigmund Freud believed or a quest for power, as Alfred Adler taught, but a quest for meaning, as said by Viktor Frankl. A meaningful life gives equal importance to all the members of the self-team, putting the skill sets of all the team members on the pedestal of living.

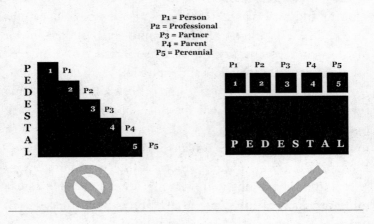

Cambridge dictionary defines 'profession' as 'any type of work that needs special training or a particular skill, often one that is respected because it requires a high level of education'. Oxford dictionary adds 'a paid occupation' to the meaning of profession. Now, we do not have higher levels of education or training for coupledom, childcare, eldercare, raising a family, parenting and perennialling. These are not even paid occupations.

We are made to believe that partnering and parenting require neither skills nor compensation. Hence, it is no coincidence that all these jobs have been assigned to women for centuries. The concept of 'P Pedestalling' advocates a change in this belief. Partnering, parenting and perennialling require a whole lot of preparation and should be acknowledged as 'meta-skills'. A meta-skill is a set of practical knowledge which can be applied to various circumstances including the ones we haven't experienced yet.

Excellence 360 degree means diving deep into the reservoir of our meta-skills as a partner (to a sibling, co-founder or a spouse) and as a parent (to a cause, a mentee, old parents or a child). The extract of life-learning concentrated in our 'partner' and 'parent' pods should be journaled and indexed for their proper projection and valuation as meta-skills.

Documentation of skills and meta-skills and putting them all on a pedestal will make an optimal life for each one of us. Being a proper father or mother is the most important thing that we can do in our lives, according to Richard Branson.[51] Valuing meta-skills, positioning them well and applying them in various domains will create a multidimensional life, where only professional success will not take the lion's share of life's worth.

---

[51]Sekulich, Tony, 'Top Five Lessons in Leadership from Richard Branson of Virgin Group', Tharawat Magazine, 18 April 2018, https://bit.ly/3wEA0Rd. Accessed on 6 May 2022.

HOW TO BE A 'P PEDESTALLER'

A 'P Pedestaller' is the one who takes equal pride in nurturing all his P pods. They bring all the pods: the person, the partner, the professional and the parent on to the centre stage of life. The action plan to become a P Pedestaller unfolds here.

Work-Life Integration, Not Work-Life Balance: During 1986–96, the media mentioned the term 'work-life balance' 32 times, while in 2007 alone, it was mentioned 1,674 times.[52] This shows that we have now started noticing the need for balance between work life and domestic life. But, before settling for this term, we need to understand what it entails. First, it means that work and life are separate. Work is lifeless and life means no work. This definition devalues our work and makes our life frivolous. There is life in work and work makes our life in all domains meaningful. To become a P Pedestaller, 'work-life balance' should be rechristened 'work-life integration'. It is imprudent to believe that work happens outside homes while life happens inside. Work actually happens in all the domains. Second, Stew Friedman, 'total leadership' professor at Wharton, says that 'balance' is a conventional but incorrect metaphor to be used with work and life. Whenever we talk of balances and scales, there is a trade-off involved, which means something needs to be subtracted from one side to be added to the other side.[53]

If more work is to be added, some life is to be subtracted

[52]Barker, Eric, 'How to Achieve Work-Life Balance in 5 Steps', *Time*, 2 April 2014, https://bit.ly/3szBUAs. Accessed on 16 May 2022.

[53]'Why Balance Is the Wrong Metaphor for Work and Life', Stern Strategy Group, 11 March 2016, https://bit.ly/3yRzLE9. Accessed on 9 May 2022.

which makes them mutually exclusive. But life is fluid. So, work and life are integrated, not separated. We need work-life harmony, not balance. If the four pillars of life are to live, to laugh, to learn and to love, can they be segregated between work and life? Don't we live and laugh while working? Don't we learn and work in life? This harmony and integration will be achieved when work at home is considered meaningful. Rather than demeaning domestic chores as drudgery or an operational hazard, we need a social flip and a mental moulding to understand the meaningfulness of work at home.

Work-life integration or integration of work in all domains is possible when we achieve two milestones. These have been discussed here.

1. Acknowledge the work experience of parents, caregivers, spouses and mentors. When their work is undervalued, they start disliking what they do, calling them 'thankless jobs', something they would like to outsource. Since these experiences are not considered worthy of adding value to professional life and life in general, men are hesitant, almost indifferent to devoting their time, energy and emotion in the domestic domain.

    Daymond John, a member of the entrepreneurial business show *Shark Tank*, and the CEO and founder of the lifestyle brand FUBU, married young and had two daughters. At the same time, he was building FUBU and working 30 hours a day. He was so busy professionally that he unwittingly thought of catching up with his daughters when they would be 10 years and later than that. He ignored his 'partner' and 'parent' piece because he was running after money. By the time his company FUBU became a $6 billion brand, his wife had decided to leave him. 'Money is not success. Money just drives your problems in a Bugatti,' philosophizes John.[54] Men think that being a husband and a father can be postponed or ignored because career advancement opportunities won't wait. Had John integrated his work across the personal and professional domains while acknowledging the contribution of his wife, he wouldn't have had a divorce, which he considers the most painful memory of his life.

This acknowledgement of work experience in the domestic domain comes with a caveat of not 'hero worshipping' those who neglect their domestic roles but become professional trendsetters.

When a modern family comprises one half excelling at work and the other half excelling at home, it is not balance. It is a distribution which is unfair and uncalled for. There is no balance of power in such a distribution.

Danish fathers strive to excel at their role as a parent by taking a long paternity leave to learn all that traditionally mothers are expected to do. A stay-at-home dad who takes as much pride in changing diapers as in filing tax returns will usher in the era of work-life integration, i.e. integration of work in all domains, not division of a mother's role and a father's role.

2. Take your 'person face' to your workplace. Work-life

[54]Clifford, Catherine, 'What "Shark Tank" investor Daymond John learned when he threw a party and nobody came', CNBC Make it, 2 November 2016, https://cnb.cx/3KdxBC9. Accessed on 22 August 2022.

integration entails not only the 'partner' and 'parent' pod to be put on a professional pedestal but also the 'person' pod. An executive should be able to go to his workplace with his real face.

Darnell Thompson worked at the IT department at Accenture, US, where he lived with his family. He heard about two police shootings of unnamed African-American men in 2016 and it disturbed him immensely as he was raising a young Black boy. He wrote a Facebook post about the unjust treatment being meted out to people like him. Ellyn Shook, Chief Leadership and HR officer at Accenture, read the post and connected with Darnell to confront him. Darnell shared, 'I am worried about my family. I am frightened for them but I come to work every day with a mask on my face and no one else is feeling what I am going through.' Ellyn was shaken and that is how the 'Building Bridges' platform was started at Accenture. This program has changed the way I think about what's possible to share at work, says organizational psychologist, Adam Grant.[55] Ellyn hosted a live webcast with Julie Sweet, Accenture's North America CEO, to have an open dialogue about race and diversity. A thousand Accenture employees from across the country shared their experiences for an hour and how it affects them at work. Today, anyone can convene a 'Building Bridges' meeting on anything, ranging from sexual discrimination and politics to faith. No topics are rejected

---

but one needs to ensure that everyone participates, listens as well as talks. One can bring an expert with him if they want help while talking about something. No one needs to be one person at home and another at work. Showing up with your 'family face' at the workplace can improve excellence manifold. Organizations can disclose themselves as integrators of personal-professional stories of their workforce or as segregators of these stories. Such self-disclosure will help in ascertaining if the organization is a P Pedestaller or not.

Tone Tag is an Indian start-up that combines data with sound technology to create software for online payment. The culture at Tone Tag has humanized this organization. On their LinkedIn profile, they post the pictures of the team singing together, voting together or snacking together. They use the hashtag #humansoftonetag. They share their stories with newcomers when they join this company. Every Tuesday, their team starts their day by singing the national anthem. The HR head feels that it empowers them, gives them a sense of belonging and pride as an Indian start-up. They meet every Tuesday (the entire team at Mumbai and Bengaluru) for 30 minutes and share updates on the personal front, discuss holidays taken, the purchase of new gadgets and celebrate small achievements.

To become a P Pedestaller, run through the marathon of life by integrating, not segmenting the different P pods. Work consists of whatever we are obliged to do. Play consists of whatever we are not obliged to do. And life happens between the two.

Welcome the 'Unheard' and 'Unseen' Perspectives:
Author Gloria Steinem, in her famous essay 'If Men Could
Menstruate', writes: 'Whatever a "superior" group has, it will
be used to justify its superiority and whatever an "inferior"
group has, that will be used to justify its plight.'[56] If men
could menstruate, it would have become an enviable,
worthy masculine event. If only men could give birth,
pregnancy would automatically get a pivotal position in the
life cycle—professional and personal. Paternity leave would
be embedded in every job like casual leaves. A crèche in
every office would be as common a feature as a washroom.
The trivialized, marginalized 'problems of pregnancy and
fatherhood' will organically take centre stage. Women would
be considered those unfortunate beings who have not been
chosen to give birth to the next generation. The 'pregnancy'
duration would become a glorious pathway that would enrich
a man and catapult him into an exulted position. A man
who just delivered a child would get a senior rank and
all the experiences around pregnancy and delivering will
get a pedestal position, making a man specially gifted after
delivering a baby.

Our culture and our lifestyle give immense importance
to everything that men use, do and say. If pregnancy moves
from the women's realm to the men's realm, it will become
the most important milestone of a man's life, demanding
proportionate attention. It would become a 'glorified
milestone' from a 'necessary evil'. It would turn into a

---

[56]Steinem, Gloria, 'If Men Could Menstruate', *Literal Latte*, www.literal-latte.com/1994/06/if-men-could-menstruate/. Accessed on 5 May 2022.

life-altering and elevating experience reserved for men. Nursing rooms and feeding breaks would be treated similar to meeting rooms and tea breaks. The way men can shave in front of women, feeding would be equally a public activity. Variety of feeding pads and pumps would have been available much earlier, in a shelf next to the after-shave lotion.

We wouldn't have to hide sanitary napkins in newspapers and black polybags. The ads would not show a blue gel-like liquid on the pads. A shaven hair is showed off with aplomb, after all. Premenstrual syndrome (PMS) would not be laughed at. There would be health initiatives like walking '10,000 steps' around it. Men would be considered stronger and women would be relegated to a much weaker position. Pregnancy, which has been justified to weaken the position of professional women, would be justified in strengthening the position of professional men.

The perspective of the powerful gains currency. To become a P Pedestaller, to practise excellence 360 degree, let the unheard and the unseen perspectives of women get heard and seen at work.

Indra Nooyi, former CEO of PepsiCo, suggested a special packaging of chips for women. She observed that women like to keep a small packet of chips in their purse and prefer chips that make a less crunchy noise on eating and does not make the fingers messy with the sticky seasoning. Her suggestions led to the making of the Doritos chips for women for the market.

Whoopi Goldberg has founded a line of non-smokable medical cannabis products, Emma and Clyde, that help women in alleviating their menstrual pain and cramps. She believes that this problem would have been solved much earlier had men faced such issues. She says, 'A friend of mine was talking about a few famous people launching marijuana lines, and I asked if anyone was doing a menstrual line, and they laughed at me. They called it a "niche market". But the niche market is half the population on earth.'[57]

It is important that women's experience be given centre stage in decisions that impact meaningfulness of life. There is a famous online list of deathbed regrets which mentions regrets of high-achieving men.

'I wish I had been more financially prudent.'

'I wish I had chosen myself over social obligations.'

'I wish I had expressed my honest opinions and needs.'

'I wish I had not worried about being accepted and approved and appreciated by others.'

The deathbed regrets of women are not mentioned online because their perspectives are not considered relevant enough. The way deathbed regrets of men motivate them to value relationships more, the documented deathbed regrets of women might propel them to be more assertive and self-confident. Surprisingly, the perspective of one half of the population doesn't get the weightage it deserves.

Similarly, perspectives and experiences of single fathers, stay-at-home husbands and depressed males must be given attention too. New state policies are needed to accommodate the changing needs of single dads and LGBT (lesbian, gay, bisexual and transgender) partnerships. Also, perspectives of

---

[57]Cox, Ana Marie, 'Whoopi Goldberg Wants to Make You Feel Better', *The New York Times*, 31 August 2016, https://nyti.ms/3LNVtfT. Accessed on 5 May 2022.

senior people are undervalued and overlooked in offices and at home which has led to the growth of longevity leaders like Ashton Applewhite and Bonnie Marcus, who push for policy changes for older women in the fields of career, care and pensions.

It is important to understand the thought process of an active, energetic 70-year-old who is not done yet, but our society and workplaces do not wish to agree. Perennial perspective needs a position on our podium, too. Not only this, the algorithmic perspective also needs to be added to the excellence 360 degree mix. Today, an online advertiser needs to cater to the taste of the Google search algorithm rather than the taste of a human being. The Google search algorithm cannot taste an ice cream, but it has a very sophisticated taste when it comes to ranking the web pages of ice cream vendors, and the most successful ice cream vendors in the world are those that the Google algorithm ranks first, not those that produce the tastiest ice creams.

With time, we need to put the perspectives of humans of all genders as well as machines on the pedestal to make lives meaningful for each one of us.

Remodel the Relation between Money and Self-Worth: A human life is valued monetarily in life and in death. When a tragedy strikes, the victims—injured, handicapped and deceased—are compensated by the government. A waiter is not compensated equally as a CEO. The prospective income of a deceased is considered while designing a compensation package in India as well as abroad.[58]

---

[58]PTI, 'Supreme Court lays down norms for computation of accident

Kenneth Feinberg, a lawyer and compensation package consultant for the US government, worked on the compensation packages of 25 senior-most professionals belonging to top companies which were given bailout assistance during the 2008 recession. Feinberg curtailed their packages and these professionals were in turmoil. He opines that the senior officials were very emotional about their pay cut because they viewed their compensation as the sole barometer of their self-worth.[59]

Unfortunately, our pay cheque reflects who we are more than our families, our children and our commitment to causes. Since we are judged by the money we make, our profession pod takes the centre stage. This way of thinking and living needs a shift, especially given the unprecedented times of climate change and the Covid-19 chaos.

Jan Dion is a Copenhagen-based garbageman. He enjoys collecting rubbish for a living because it allows him to work only for five hours a day and then he can spend the rest of his time with his family and coaching his daughter's handball team. Jan is happy as a professional, a parent, a partner and a person. Since he is not judged for his job choice in Denmark, the self-worth is not connected to what he does and how much he earns.[60]

Famous Hollywood producer Michael Ovitz sums up his

claim', *The Economic Times*, 31 October 2017, https://bit.ly/3TjZWv5. Accessed on 22 August 2022.

[59]'Who Decides How Much a Life Is Worth?', Freakonomics, https://bit.ly/3lbEusf. Accessed on 16 May 2022.

[60]Wier, Bill and Sylvia Johnson, 'Denmark: The Happiest Place on Earth', AbcNews, 8 January 2009.

life by saying, 'Had I won a little less by being less competitive and less immersed in my profession, it would have been fine.' This galloping ahead merely with the 'professional' cape, leaving behind the 'partnerial' and 'parental' gowns gaping, is actually an idea of self-sabotage in the long run.

Laura Nash and Howard Stevenson, the authors of *Just Enough*, say that money is pretty easy to count and it brings some happiness for a short period of time. Though friends, family and love are equally important, they are complicated and cannot be delivered by Amazon Prime. While ignoring these immeasurable complexities, people follow a 'collapsing' strategy—collapsing everything into one barometer of the money yardstick—which eventually fails to evaluate one's self-worth.[61]

We can live our lives by maximizing or satisficing. While the former is to explore various options, weigh them and strive for the best possible, the latter is knowing one's need and picking what is good enough. Our self-worth should not be defined by maximizing professionally but by satisficing in all the roles. Money is an integral part of self-worth but not the *only* part.

Create a 'P' Index: Academic achievements in the form of grades have clarity. Professional achievement in the form of pay packages and promotions is transparent and measurable. Measurable outcomes are easy to understand and glib to talk about. These achievements and their consequences are visible and tangible, while investment of time, emotions

---

[61]Barker, Eric, *Barking up the Wrong Tree: the Surprising Science behind Why Everything You Know about Success Is (Mostly) Wrong*, HarperOne, 2019.

and effort in building a marriage or raising a child doesn't give concrete and immediate outcome. First, a rock-solid marriage cannot be measured. Even if it is valued, no one wants to credit any one person for the solidarity. Second, a successful marriage or a confident, responsible child is not valued as much as the economic status of a family. Partnering and parenting roles are rendered powerless due to our fixation with the professional and personal roles. Our economic mindset finds all the meaning in earning. Earning 'meaning' in life is not the priority if it emanates from parenting or partnering. The people who design work policy and public policy around quality of life value gross domestic product (GDP) more than MDP (meaning-driven parenting or partnering).

Noted economist Amartya Sen believes that each person should get a life worthy of her human dignity. He introduced the theory of capability, which states that all the theories of well-being focus narrowly on a few things. He worries about people getting 'normalized' to their condition of material deprivation and social injustice, especially women and old folks.[62] His two arguments are important here. First, suppose a household owns a cycle, which would mean that they have an answer to their transportation problem. The world will perceive them as having a facility to stay mobile. But each member of the household might not have access to it. An old or handicapped family member might be physically disabled to use it and women might be socially disabled to use it. In

---

[62]'Sen's Capability Approach', Internet Encyclopaedia of Philosophy, https://iep.utm.edu/sen-cap/. Accessed on 16 May 2022.

this case, the cycle doesn't actually improve their 'movement' well-being. Similarly, if women's perspectives are neither documented nor valued, it hurts their overall well-being.

Second, a country's GDP denotes the quality of life of its people. But this lopsided unit of measurement cannot denote anything about the emotional or spiritual quality of people's life. It does not take into account the quality of life of every individual in the household.

'Leaders of countries often focus on national economic growth alone, while their people are striving for something different: meaningful lives for themselves,' says Martha Nussbaum.[63]

We need to create a 'P' index that helps in measuring the performance and learning of a person in the roles of a professional, partner, parent and a person. A sample 'P' index can be used to assess the following competencies through an external appraisal.

Person	*Professional*	*Partner*	*Parent*
Authenticity	Ambition	Shared Context	Persuasion
Creativity	Acumen	Power Balance	Egolessness
Humility	Commitment	Love	Observation

Weak performance in any of these roles will lead to a weak 'P' index. A good enough performance in all will be considered better than exceptional performance in one and dismal

---

[63]Nussbaum, Martha C., *Creating Capabilities – The Human Development Approach,* Harvard University Press; Reprint edition (2013).

performance in the rest. This will help men and women who wish to lead an excellent 360 degree life. All the working men would wish to remain loving partners and involved parents to score well on the P index. It will nudge the unidimensional men and women to think holistically about their lives. All the working women will not feel the guilt trip while staying at home since their parenting experience will not become a gap on the résumé. Women will feel more confident and empowered when the energy and emotions invested in the family will be valued at the professional level. All the PROTIPs will stay relevant professionally as they would be able to showcase how their partner and parental selves are contributing to their professional selves when they decide to make a professional comeback. Every individual will get a voice and a value when he has a 'P' index valuation. Children would be educated to sharpen their overall competencies, making them rounded individuals. This will make all the domestic jobs meaningful. A 'P' index will catalyse mechanical, thoughtless activities into valuable experiences. There are standardized tests to test intelligence but not to measure wisdom. Just because we haven't devised methods to measure wisdom, it doesn't become less valuable. A 'P' index could be a step in that direction.

Add 'Soft Talents' or 'Meta-Skills' to the Vocabulary: The way communication skills, leadership skills, time management, and cognitive or emotional skills are called 'soft skills' and are highly sought after by employers, we need the cluster of partnering, parenting and eldercare to be recognized as 'soft-talents'. As soft skills improve our likeability and employability, soft talents too improve life quality and dignity. Soft talents must have a skin in the game of life. An individual can be a 'holistic hero' only when he is a champion of 'soft talents' or 'meta-skills.'

Laura Nash and Howard Stevenson conducted an exhaustive research amongst successful professionals, executives and Harvard Business School graduates through interviews, surveys, model-testing sessions and conversations with people from different walks of life at every level of the economy. They wanted to find the components of lasting or enduring success—success that is emotionally renewing and sustainable beyond being momentarily rewarding.[64]

They uncovered four irreducible components of enduring success:

- Happiness: Feelings of pleasure or contentment about your life.
- Achievement: Challenges that give a sense of accomplishment.
- Significance: Sense of positively impacting the people we care for.
- Legacy: A way to establish your values or accomplishments so as to help others find future success.

Laura and Howard believe that all the four components are essential for enduring success. Take away any one component and it no longer feels like 'real' success. They stress that unless you hit all the four categories with regularity, any

[64]Nash, Laura and Howard H. Stevenson, 'Success That Lasts', *Harvard Business Review*, 1 August 2014, hbr.org/2004/02/success-that-lasts. Accessed on 5 May 2022.

one win will fail to satisfy in the long run. That is what 'P Pedestalling' means—regularly putting all our roles on the pedestal to feel happy, accomplished, significant and legendary while shuffling between different roles. The baseline for these individuals was not the amount of activity or number of rewards in any one category, but the securing of a proportionate mix of all five.

BRIANA WILLIAMS: I DID IT ALL BECAUSE I COULD

She is a young woman who graduated from Harvard Law School in 2018, with a baby girl in tow. Briana Williams, through her choices, is persistent to take all the Ps of her life to the podium without any self-doubt, guilt or arrogance.

Coming from a very humble background, Briana could not secure admission in school once because her family, being homeless, could not present an address proof. She and her boyfriend had been together for almost a decade when she joined Harvard Law School. Many law scholars had their families around in the campus, so having a baby didn't feel like a foolish idea to her. However, their partnership turned sour when she had just transitioned into the first phase of motherhood.

Talking about her tumultuous but triumphant journey, she reminisces, 'From the boldest of inquiries, this question even manifested into a censure of my reproductive choice, as I was asked, "Why didn't you decide to get an abortion?" Well, the reason that I decided to continue to pursue my career and legal degree at Harvard while transitioning into motherhood is quite simple: I could.'[65]

Briana agrees that women are thought to be successful at one thing only, thus trashing the idea of her ability to achieve both professional and familial success as being impossible. She shares with pride that she was unwavering in both her classroom and parenting obligations.

She took her daughter to classes or to meetings with professors. Also, she worked on an essay while in labour. She neither missed any doctor's appointment nor any college deadline. She missed out on some sleep for sure. 'I proved myself to me' is her anthem. She has learned as much, perhaps more, from her experiences as a mother as she has in her Harvard classrooms. By not allowing any opinions or archetypes to define her, she has brought her parenthood and her professionalism to the centre stage, without guilt or embarrassment or fear.

P PEDESTALLING NUGGETS

- Delete work-life balance, download work-life integration.
- Do not hero-worship professionals who perform suboptimally as a partner and as a parent.
- Show up at your workplace with your real person face.
- Whip a flip at work to hear the 'unheard' and see the 'unseen' perspectives of women and men as people, partners, parents and perennials.
- Look at the relationship between money and self-worth

---

[65]'Briana Williams: How I graduated from Harvard Law School at 24 as a single mom', Fox23 News, https://bit.ly/3G36Tuh. Accessed on 16 May 2022.

with fresh eyes. In this post Covid-19 era, you will witness a paradigm shift.

- Campaign to create a P index, which has the potential to become a part of the human development index.
- Acknowledge meta-skills of partnering, parenting and eldercare as soft talents, the way we acknowledge soft skills. The former improves the quality and dignity of life, while the latter improves one's employability.
- Put all the P pods of your self-team on the pedestal of life so that each one of them gets a voice and value, thereby, making life worth living for all.

TRANSFER LEARNING

THE MAN WHO LEARNS FROM ATTITUDES AS WELL AS ALGORITHMS

While researching and framing my thoughts for the excellence 360 degree concept, I wrote a small post on LinkedIn. I tagged a person whose thoughts and principles have always resonated with me. For me, he is a person, professional, partner, parent and perennial par excellence. On the post, he commented: 'I couldn't agree more.' The post became viral and my confidence grew manifold.[66]

It is difficult to find people like American investor Ray Dalio, who can lead such a wholesome life and share it all with honesty and radical transparency. As a person, professional, partner, parent and perennial, his learnings,

---

[66]Lodha, Dr Swati. https://bit.ly/3PQnPr2. Accessed on 28 August 2022.

accumulated over years of experience, have the potential to transform our lives completely. Dalio is a thinker-doer-sharer, the owner of one of the top US-based investment firms Bridgewater Associates, a deeply immersed partner and a parent to four boys.

He started working at the tender age of eight because he loved it more than merely memorizing what they were being taught in school. He distributed newspapers, mowed lawns, shovelled snow off people's driveways, caddied, bussed tables and washed dishes at a local restaurant before he started to play the stock market at the age of 12. He learnt many investment lessons—good, bad and ugly—in his school and college years before joining Harvard Business School in 1971. On a blind date, he met Barbara, a Spanish woman who barely spoke English. Still, they communicated in other ways, eventually got married and have had a successful partnership till date. After working for two years with some hedge fund companies, Dalio founded Bridgewater Associates with a friend and a young assistant from his two-bedroom apartment.

As a professional, he made models like back-of-the-envelope sketches, and analysed and converted them into computer programs with the technology he could afford then.[67] He created standard practices by merging human thinking with algorithms to get the best of both worlds. It helped him make unbiased but humanized decisions. He has explicitly written principles to deal with different situations arising at Bridgewater.

---

[67]Dalio, Ray, *Principles: Life and Work*, Simon and Schuster, 2017.

The three fundamental principles at the core of Bridgewater Associates—idea meritocracy, radical transparency and believability-weighted decision-making—can transform our lives as a person, partner and parent too.

At Bridgewater, the largest hedge fund in the world, no one believes in democracy or autocracy, it is idea meritocracy from top to bottom. Idea meritocracy needs radical truthfulness and radical transparency. We shy away from being radically truthful and transparent even with our spouse and children, while it is the norm in this organization employing 2,000 people.

Adam Grant, the noted organizational psychologist and author, candidly says that he has worked with hundreds of organizations and has found only one, Bridgewater, where 'criticism' is truly the norm.[68] At Bridgewater, it is clearly conveyed to every employee that criticism is meant to help you. Even if it hurts in the moment, it is going to be beneficial in the long run, just like exercising. So, they are encouraged to keep at it.

Only those who buy into the importance of a thoughtful disagreement, the routine of being criticized and evaluated openly and the norm of feeling good on being proven wrong or criticized manage to build their careers at Bridgewater.

Jim Haskel, someone who works for Dalio, reportedly wrote him an email, 'Ray, you deserve a D—for your performance today in the meeting… You didn't prepare well at all because there is no way you could have been that

---

[68]Grant, Adam, 'How to Love Criticism', LinkedIn, 20 April 2018, https://bit.ly/3sCf3nw. Accessed on 16 May 2022.

disorganized.'[69] This kind of feedback from an employee to an owner is rare—not because it is rarely possible but because it is rarely acceptable. At Bridgewater Inc., everyone is encouraged to express their views regardless of their position in the company. Bridgewater works on a Dot Collector app that collects opinions of all the concerned workers on a specific question as dots and then the data is passed through various algorithms in a computer that is watching all these people.[70]

It keeps a watch on what people are thinking, correlates that with how they think and then communicates advice back to them. Then it draws the data from all the meetings to create a pointillist picture of what people are like and how they think. It helps them to eliminate what Dalio considers the biggest tragedies of mankind—people arrogantly, naively holding on to opinions that are wrong and act on them rather than publicly stress test them.

Dalio transfers the same philosophy to his other P pods ensuring radical transparency in his relationships too. Bridgewater is proof that the quest for business excellence and the search for personal realization need not be mutually exclusive, and can in fact, be essential to each other, says Harvard psychologist Bob Kegan.[71] Bridgewater has developed some tools and apps that form the bedrock of its culture to standardize human behaviour and decision-making. These

---

[69]Montag, Ali, 'Billionaire Ray Dalio: Bridgewater's radically transparent culture evolved from "painful mistakes"', CNBC Make It, 13 September 2017, https://cnb.cx/3PUQH1v. Accessed on 22 August 2022.

[70]Ibid.

[71]Dalio, Ray, *Principles: Life and Work*, Simon & Schuster; Illustrated edition, 2017, p. 76.

tools are a combination of thoughts and technology, the unison of attitudes and algorithms, the mix of creative and artificial intelligence.

Similar to the Dot Collector app that collects the behaviour of every individual in a group and helps everyone see the thought processes of others too during the discussion, they have created Baseball Cards, which present a person's strengths and weaknesses backed by evidence. These cards are useful in meetings, where they allow people to assess the qualities of whosoever is expressing a point of view to examine the merit of that opinion. Earlier, people were worried that these cards would pigeonhole people unfairly. However gradually, people found that information out in the open was more liberating than constraining. It gave them the same comfort in the office that they enjoyed with the family, at home.

Imagine, how a P Card, on the same lines as a Baseball Card, can help discover how far a person is from holistic heroism or how they can better their performance in a specific role. As a supplement to Baseball Cards, Bridgewater has developed another tool called People Profile, which takes all the data from Baseball Cards to provide a text summary of how an employee is perceived by people at Bridgewater. Then, the self-perception of the person concerned is also integrated with it. Then extracting the qualities of a person from these Baseball Cards, they are matched to jobs using the combinators, which helps in creating job specifications and in aligning them with the right person. Imagine how it can help PROTIPs get into new jobs if their partnership and parenting experiences during 'stay-at-home' period could

be transferred to the professional learning using a P Card.
For example: a new mother develops more patience and
empathy and better time-management skills. Over time, she
learns new ways of negotiation and conflict resolution while
handling her children. If these learnings are documented on
a P Card as experience while staying out of a job, there will
be no break in career or a gap on one's résumé.

Bridgewater has also created an Issue Log for recording
the mistakes of employees and learning from them. Dalio
says that it acts like a water filter that catches garbage. This
log provides an effective metrics of performance as the
problems are logged in with the people responsible for it.
It helps in changing habits and perceptions. Since radical
transparency is the norm, employees do not hesitate to openly
point out mistakes. Imagine how an issue log could solve
issues between partners and parents if radical transparency
can be acculturated.

Another interesting tool is a Pain Button. Dalio
propounds that Pain + Reflection = Progress. When we
reflect on what caused us pain and learn from it, we progress.
The Pain Button allows an employee to record their pain
the moment they experience it. It allows the employees to
record their emotions there and then, but it doesn't allow
them to reflect at that time. The tool prompts users who
experience the pain to specify what steps they will take to
avoid this pain in the future. It guides people to reflect with
the help of questions and also record the frequency of their
using the Pain Button and the results produced. This button
is always available.

Imagine how such a button could help teenagers and their

parents resolve their generational issues if the family culture revolves around candour and long-term understanding. Dalio's pioneering work as a professional can have deep footprints in different chambers of our lives because his learnings can be transferred to other realms as well.

As a person, he swears by a great character, common sense and creativity. His principles aim at building these qualities, apart from creating meaningful work and meaningful relationships. He believes in excellence and hence is known as being tough on people. He tries to ensure problems are brought to the surface, and their root causes diagnosed which assures continuous improvement.

When Ross Waller, the in-charge of the trading department at Bridgewater, forgot to put in a trade for a client, it made a loss of several hundred thousand dollars. Instead of firing Waller, Dalio used the occasion to implement a new approach at Bridgewater. Ross and he worked to create an Error Log in the trading department which led to the adoption of the Issue Log throughout Bridgewater. He insisted that if a mistake happened and it was logged, it was fine. If it was hidden and not logged, one was in trouble.

As a parent, Dalio has been radically transparent about his son Paul's bipolar disorder, which led him to extremes of behaviour. He was jailed for violent behaviour, admitted to the psychiatric ward of a hospital, got into smoking marijuana and drinking before they could bring him back with the help of psychologists and caregivers. Because of his experiences with Paul, he empathized with people who saw and did things differently. This understanding that people are wired differently got transferred to his professional chamber, making him a far better and effective leader.

He became a parent to his small company much before he became a father. He considers the decision of becoming a father the most difficult, yet the best. As a parent, mentor and perennial, Dalio loves to pass on the knowledge, he feels that passing on knowledge is like passing on DNA. For him, learning and helping others learn is the core of a life well-lived, with radical open mindedness and radical transparency.

Dalio believed that he was doing two distinct jobs simultaneously all his life—building his business and being a good father, husband and friend. He realized that the demands of these roles changed over time and so he changed his skills and abilities accordingly.

As a partner, Dalio has teamed up with friends who have been a part of his organization and family from day one. Barbara Dalio works passionately to help students in the most stressed public-school districts in Connecticut and she and their son Matt have opened the doors of philanthropy for Dalio.

Greg Jensen, who he had mentored for two decades, has taken up the CEO's role—not any of his sons because they have had different creative interests.

As a perennial, at the age of 72, Dalio is focused on the next phase of his life—pursuing his passions and helping others succeed—with the help of his book *Principles: Life and Work* and with his new 'PrinciplesYou' assessment which helps people learn about themselves.[72]

---

[72]Scipioni, Jade, 'Billionaire Ray Dalio on his routine-free life, what keeps him up at night and his next chapter', CNBC Make It, 11 May 2021, https://cnb.cx/3NTGfGh. Accessed on 22 August 2022.

He has always taken advice from the people who have excelled in a specific field. For philanthropic investments, he learnt from Bill and Melinda Gates, Warren Buffett and the Omidyar folks. He learnt a lot about geniuses like Steve Jobs and Einstein from Walter Isaacson. He consulted several management thinkers like Jim Collins when his succession plan didn't succeed. Thus, Dalio's life is a masterclass in learning—transferring it, passing it and evolving it.

WHAT IS TRANSFER LEARNING?

As a recap of the chapter on self-teaming, let us recall the four pods residing in each one of us.

These four P pods form human beings, the way pea pods form a pea. Each pod has some potential competencies which they can own and hone, or neglect and forget. Each one of us evolves by catalysing one, two or all P pods, sequentially or simultaneously. We are culturally conditioned to acknowledge one or two of the pods while neglecting the rest, while excellence 360 degree is an attempt to run the marathon of life with maximum possible Ps in tow.

To excel at running this marathon, each P pod should first sharpen the competencies that it has.

After enhancing the existing knowledge two things should happen. First, each pod must transfer its learnings to the other pods. Second, each pod must learn from external resources to enrich and upgrade itself consistently. Thus, after strengthening the core competencies of each pod, excellence 360 degree advocates 'intrinsic transfer learning' and 'extrinsic transfer learning'. The former happens in the inner classroom, where each member of a self-team can teach the rest a thing or two. It requires a constant back and forth between different P pods. The latter happens when the external people excelling in various fields infuse their learnings into different P pods.

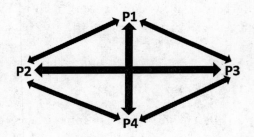

Internal Transfer Learning

For people to effectively navigate from a professional pod to a partner pod, or vice versa, a constant calibration is needed. To efficiently play the different roles that are important to us, which impact our lives daily, we need to switch from one pod to another to start each conversation on a clean slate.

Say, for instance, you come back from office after a stressful day that left you feeling inadequate or tired. However, you need to switch your partner mode on as you reach home. It is a conscious move to recalibrate the pessimism into a smile, an openness to absorb the energy of the house. If your partner also had a tough day at home or at work, same calibration from his/her side will help. Even if it is missing, it will at least keep the volatility or negative energy lower that what it would have been if you too entered with your state of unhappiness. You need to consciously switch on the parent mode to observe and listen to your child as you meet them rather than passing on your irritation on seeing his messy room. Your emotion of helplessness or anger from work can get accentuated when you see a dirty napkin or a child's messy room. This happens in families on a regular basis and is completely unwarranted. The dynamics of different roles are different and a slow, conscious movement is needed. If you pick up a call from your son during a high-stress business meeting and you forget to recalibrate to your parent mode, it might dent the child's excitement or urgency that made him call you. Mind it, this is not fake, this is not putting on an act, this is conscious calibration because a child calling to share something or to ask something doesn't need to get hit by the stress of your work.

In his book *Psyched Up: How the Science of Mental Preparation Can Help You Succeed*, Daniel McGinn, senior editor at *Harvard Business Review*, talks about a neurosurgeon Mark McLaughlin, who was a wrestler in school and followed a routine taught by a sports psychologist that involved visualization and some exercises.[73] When he started operating as a surgeon, he realized that it is as high pressure a job as wrestling. So, he uses the same process where he listens to his favourite music for, say, four minutes before starting the operation, pushes a chair to the corner, scrubs

---

[73]'Mental Preparation Secrets of Top Athletes, Entertainers, and Surgeons,' *Harvard Business Review*, 18 June 2018.

quietly and keeps an old set of operating equipment used by his mentor on the tray (he doesn't use them). He consciously monitors the amount of caffeine he takes to stay alert.

It corresponds with my personal experience. Before a talk or training, I look at my notes for four to five minutes, put on a big watch, wear a saree and talk to myself about how I felt during my last talk. After the talk, as I get into the car, I transition from my professional pod to the personal one. I take stock of my feelings, talk to family and friends or listen to some podcast, with a smile on my face. (My driver is used to it by now.) As I reach home, I consciously come out of the personal space to transition into the partner/parent pod. The transition involves coating my mind with patience if my husband and daughter are expected to be home together or keep my mind open for any surprise. It helps to give a 30-second talk to prime yourself into the next pod of the hyper loop. 'Looking back' and 'looking forward' both help in priming ourselves into playing the role.

Reflecting and visualizing help prepare the mind for entering the pod. For instance, if you used a pep talk to pacify the fears of your anxious 12-year-old last time and he told you to shut up, you can reflect and then imagine that you need a different strategy to deal with the child. Maybe, priming yourself to be an empathetic sponge will work where you restrict your talk to 'I know', and lot of genuine nodding.

A daily periodical 'psyching up' is needed for us to play these different roles in a continuum every day. Alison Wood Brooks, assistant professor at Harvard Business School, opines that it is personally empowering for her to embrace the idea of having multiple selves. She says that she cannot be the same person when she is in front of her executive education class, when she is at home with her young kids and when she is attending a bachelorette party in Las Vegas. She emphasizes that they are all 'authentically me' (I added the inverted commas for emphasis) but she is not being a single consistent human across all these various contexts.[74]

HOW TO BE A TRANSFER LEARNER

When a girl morphs into a professional from being a student, she embraces the professional garb completely as she doesn't need to travel back to being the student. But when she interns during her degree course, she needs to keep the shifting mode on. When she marries, she adds another role that needs to be attended to every day. A disciplinarian at work might need to be a relaxed partner. She needs to realize that she needs to shift her orientation. 'Get the work done' approach that works wonders at the workplace will not bring out the best in her as a spouse. She needs to focus on her daily agility to retrieve the 'passionate partner' from her 'disciplined professional'. This agile role shifting from professional to partner and back, from partner to parent and back, is what life expects from us. This P2P movement on a daily basis requires mental alertness as well as effortlessness of execution. Don't get the impression that a man doesn't need to be a part of this 'back and forth'. In order to create an

---

[74]'Introducing Dear HBR:', *Harvard Business Review*, 7 June 2018, hbr.org/ideacast/2018/02/introducing-dear-hbr. Accessed on 5 May 2022.

excellence-infused life, the shift of professional orientation to become an equal partner and an involved parent is a must.

Let us understand how internal transfer learning takes place:

1. **Lessons from the 'Parent in You' to other Ps:** There are certain experiences which surely take place in the domain of parents and hence, they can extend the learning to other pods. As explained earlier, the parent pod inherently has seeds of persuasion, egolessness, patience and observation. In the context of multidimensional wholesome living by practising excellence 360 degree, here are the most appropriate definitions of seeds and how they would transfer their learnings to other pods.

   a) **Persuasion:** The parent pod cradles persuasion which, as Aristotle suggested, has three core ingredients: logos or logic, ethos or ethic and pathos or emotion. On acknowledging and catalysing the P pod, an individual would develop their reasoning ability as coherent, personality as credible and content as emotional. It is pertinent to consistently persuade children or mentees towards the task at hand. The sooner one begins practising persuasion, the earlier one begins to marry logic with emotion.

   How to transfer persuasion to other pods: An effective parent of today needs to be patiently persuasive for a span of two decades across various trajectories of life. A parent nudges himself/herself to stay patient and focussed with the task at hand while nudging the child towards the same. Parents of ace shuttler and coach P. Gopichand have persisted and used persuasion not only as parents but also as people, professionals and partners. Subbaravamma, Gopichand's mother, never compromised with a disciplined routine for Gopi since childhood and it remains a habit with him till today. For a four-year-old Gopi in Chennai, she would negotiate with older boys that unless he was given equal participation in playing outdoors, she would not allow either of her children to play.[75]

Subhash, Gopi's father, stood by him since he was a two-year-old, as he observed his interest in sports and an athletic mindset. Throughout the two decades of consistent training, they ensured that he got what he needed: food, shoes, shuttles, travel facilities, trainers, love and support.

The family lived a frugal life. Their moral strength led Gopi to donate a prize money of ₹40,000 for earthquake victims even when his family needed the money too. As partners, they struggled together and shared the family vision. When Gopi had a knee surgery in Delhi and they were staying in a building that had no elevators, his father carried him on his shoulders every day for his exercise routine at the hospital. Both of them have given unflinching strength to Gopi's idea of building a world-class badminton academy using their logos, ethos and pathos over the years. Both parents are active at

---

[75]Sharma, Sanjay and Shachi S. Sharma, *Pullela Gopi Chand: The World beneath His Feat*, Rupa Publications India, 2011.

the academy and have persuaded themselves to be effective in all the roles, each day.

Subhash and Subbaravamma used persistence and persuasion in all the other roles that they played over a long span of time. This internal transfer learning has influenced all the roles and realms of their life with positive persuasion. Apart from internal transfer learning, there is a great deal of external transfer learning that happens between us. Nadella the parent can help us become observant, while Nadella the professional can inspire us to scale up our empathy.

b) **Egolessness:** A seed that only a parent pod can effortlessly develop is that of being egoless, putting others before oneself. It requires the parent pod to put him/her in other's shoes and take oneself less seriously. Prioritizing others and discounting oneself helps one become considerate, sensitive and unconditionally loving to others. Though easier said than done, an ego erosion practised by the parent pod can make the lives of the next generation happier and secure. It will help parents curb their anger, thus preventing children from being the softest targets. It will also help them develop a sense of humour as they take themselves less seriously and encourage their children to do the same.

How to transfer egolessness to other pods: Parents of yore remained self-righteous and expected obedience from their children. Today, they need to be authentic and vulnerable by accepting their own drawbacks and demons in front of their children in order to have a close bond with them. Children disagree, debate and defy, keeping obedience at bay. A parent of today is a rare mix of a saint, a strategist and a psychologist, whose ego gets eroded as the children grow up.

As professionals and partners, we must learn to keep our ego in check. The lesser ego a parent exercises, the healthier their relationship is with the child. Ego erosion allows a parent to embrace his imperfections in front of his children and admit his flaws without feeling small. A 'zero ego' parent doesn't exercise authority over their children and effortlessly bridges the generation gap. All parents must embrace 'ego erosion' trait and then transfer it to the other P pods.

David Axelrod, founder of the Institute of Politics at University of Chicago, is a journalist, political strategist and a podcast host, best known for being the mastermind behind the election campaigns of Barack Obama. Axelrod acknowledged and embraced an emotional wound 31 years after it was inflicted upon him. He could feel the pain as a 19-year-old, but he could process it much later, after he became a father. When he was 19, his father, a trained psychologist, who had helped save many lives, died by suicide. His father had a tormented childhood and an unhappy marriage. He never shared his anxieties and tried to fight his demons alone. Axelrod did the same. He never spoke about losing a father to depression because it felt like a character flaw, a defect in his father, and hence, in him. He hoarded the wound, never trying to heal it. He opened the wound when he realized his pain as a father whose daughter suffered from epilepsy since birth. The medical expenses were high and he started his own political consultancy firm to make ends meet. He remained an absent father while his wife Susan Landau, a learned individual, focussed on keeping her daughter alive and functioning.

Axelrod wrote about his father to understand himself as a father and the act of writing made him authentic enough to admit his flaws as a father.[76] The ego erosion took some time, but it only happened due to his experiences as a son and a father which dissipated into other roles.

c) **Observation:** The parent pod nurtures the seed of observation by following all the steps to observe well: pay attention, make mental or physical notes, pay attention again, describe the experience, gather information from other sources and summarize one's thoughts. Parents acquire special observation skills that are silent and strategic. They observe silently because their hurried and harried responses can irreversibly harm their bond with their child. They observe strategically to pick up all the hidden keys to the feelings, fears and fantasies of their children.

---

[76]Axelrod, David, 'The Truth about My Father's Death,' *Chicago Tribune*, 16 June 2006, https://bit.ly/3R1BiND. Accessed on 22 August 2022.

How to transfer observation to other pods: Temple Grandin, a child who showed all signs of being autistic at the age of three, could earn a PhD and become the most successful animal behaviour expert because her mother Eustacia was not ready to give up on her. Autistic kids need a lot of one-to-one support in their early formative years so that they do not recede into isolation. Her mother made sure that Temple gets to talk and engage in activities she enjoys. She was made to learn table manners and she learnt it when pushed constantly.

Eustacia observed that her daughter was comfortable with animals and machines, so she put her in riding class and model rocket groups. Eustacia sent her to the ranch of her sister-in-law since she knew of Temple's love for horses and that changed her life. She realized that she enjoyed being with animals more than humans. Not only this, she discovered that cattle were like her, similarly unsettled by unexpected sounds and motions. Temple observed that the squeeze chute helped the horses calm down. Therefore, she requested her aunt to let her use it and the result was a dramatic soothing of Temple's nerves. Temple has used her visual memory and researched animal behaviour. She has changed the livestock industry of the US by redesigning slaughterhouses and working for better conditions of cattle. She teaches at Colorado State University and is hailed as a parenting guru by parents of autistic children. Had Eustacia, like her husband, given up on Temple, we would not have experienced the distinct contributions of her daughter.

Eustacia Cutler's observation skills as a mother led her to do extensive research on autism and other disabilities, through which she created prize-winning documentaries and wrote a book titled *A Thorn in My Pocket: Temple Grandin's Mother Tells the Family Story*. Not only this, her book *Autism: Old as Time* describes her journey of coming to terms with autism and how she discovered her ever- evolving capacity to renew herself.[77] Her acute observations as a parent changed her as a person and a professional, leading her to inspire many people impacted by autism.

2. **Lessons from the 'Partner in You' to other Ps:** The partner pod of a self-team prepares itself for partnering in various relationships and ventures. The skill set readied in the partner pod helps the other pods to value these skills and embrace them when needed. As explained in the chapter 'Self Teaming', the partner pod inherently has seeds of shared context, balance of power and love. Here is what these seeds mean and how to internally transfer their abilities to other pods.

a) **Shared context:** Every partnership—personal, professional and social—acknowledges its 'coming together' by specifying the reasons for that

---

[77]Cutler, Eustacia, *A Thorn in My Pocket: Temple Grandin's Mother Tells the Family Story*, Future Horizons; 1st edition, 2012.

amalgamation. For this purpose, the partner pod should be ready to answer the question: how do I build collective vision and collective goals? The partner pod should prepare itself to look for reasons that will bring commitment to that collective vision. Without readiness for sharing a context of coming together, partnership will neither last nor prosper. As a professional and a parent, we are expected to be exemplary, while all partnerships are founded on equality. It is a co-created journey of mutual trust and respect, devoid of ego and envy.

How to transfer shared context to other pods: A shared context that builds trust and respect and subtracts ego and envy is the building block of every partnership. Each one of us should be ready with a 'shared context' toolkit before making a friend, teaming with a co-founder, bringing in a pet or entering into the pact of marriage.

Let us have candid conversations early on so that we encourage our children and ourselves to excel not only in academics but in nurturing and sustaining relationships. Condoleezza Rice, former US Secretary of State, is a noted strategist who favours policy, not politics. She is known to have successfully worked with presidents George W. Bush (Senior and Junior). She was the Russia specialist with Bush Senior when he told her that his son wanted to run for the presidency. He also suggested she spend some time with him discussing foreign policy. Rice says that she hit it off immediately with

Bush Junior because 'we shared our view of the America that we wanted to live in'.[78]

Partners teach us to build a shared context in the culture of a family, a start-up or an organization. Once the sense of trusted togetherness takes over the sense of individuality, partnerships stand the test of time. Valentin Chmerkovskiy, a dancer and winner of the World Dance Championship, believes that his performance depends greatly on his equation with his partner. He said, 'I am going to make her look the best and I will help her bring out her best. My performance makes every girl in the audience to think: "Oh! She looks like a queen. How nice it must be to dance with him." When I think about my partner first, my performance and partnership excel.'[79] Thus, the partner pod internally propagates a shared context full of trust and respect, devoid of envy and ego.

b) **Balance of Power:** Power is control over social, material, psychological and reproductive resources. In the game of power, the powerful is the one who brings the most resources to the table. He becomes the influencer. The powerless is the one who believes that the influencer has control over their opinions

---

[78]'The Axe Files with David Axelrod', Ep. 208 - Condoleezza Rice, https://bit.ly/3lc71h5. Accessed on 16 May 2022.

[79]'Valentin Chmerkovskiy: The Art of Dance, Success and Pursuing Your Dreams', Lewis Howes, 17 January 2018, https://bit.ly/3MWkNQQ. Accessed on 6 May 2022.

and can inflict pain, physically or emotionally. He becomes the influenced. In any partnership, this inequation between the powerful and the powerless, the influencer and the influenced, rocks the boat. The partner pod needs to propagate equality of exercising power related to all life decisions. An authentic long-term partnership requires a robust understanding that balance of power, not dominance or control by one, can keep it going and growing.

In a marriage, a person whose partner pod acknowledges this seed of balance would ensure that it is equally maintained while making any decision: economic, emotional or erotic. In a team too, members with a catalysed partner pod would work with mutual respect for all the members who bring knowledge, skills and capital to their venture.

How to transfer balance of power to other pods: As a seven-year-old child, noted tennis player Andre Agassi hated tennis. He loved soccer, but his adamant dad hammered in his head every day that he needed to be a tennis player, that he needed to be number one and make a lot of money. Andre's mother and elder brother submitted in front of his dad and so did he. The father nagged Philly, the elder one, for not being as talented a tennis player as needed to become a champion and forced him to become a champion at any cost. Andre felt powerless, and the same vulnerability showed up in his relationship, sometimes as uncontrolled rage, sometimes as shame.[80]

Contrary to Andre's dad, who used all his power to dominate and control his family, the father of ace Indian tennis player, Sania Mirza, observed his young daughter's interest in the game and changed the course of his family's life such that it aligned with her passion for the sport. He gave a lot of power to young Sania which transferred the 'balance of power' in all the roles that she played. Sania's dad had to suddenly migrate to the US as his green card, which was applied a decade earlier by his brother and sister settled there, came through. After trying to settle down in Ohio, he realized that his four-year-old desperately wanted to take tennis lessons, which he could not afford in the foreign land. He decided to return to Hyderabad and enrolled her immediately into swimming, tennis and roller-skating. Given the power early on, Sania has successfully balanced power in her marriage, as a parent and also with her doubles' partners on the tennis court.

c) **Love:** The partner pod must not imbibe the faulty definition of love being a feeling, manifesting instinctively. It must catalyse love with all its ingredients: care, affection, recognition, respect, commitment, trust and open communication.

Bell Hooks (pseudonym for Gloria Jean Watkins), an authority on love, opines that learning faulty

---

[80]Agassi, Andre, *Open: An Autobiography*, Vintage; Reprint edition, 2010.

definitions of love when we are quite young makes it difficult to be loving as we grow older. Let the partner pod understand that love, abuse and neglect cannot coexist at any age.

Let the partner pod imbibe that love is a verb, an action, in every relation, which needs to be practised over and over again. As Esther Perel puts it: marriage is about falling in love with the same person every day. Let the pod always assert that there is no love without respect in any relationship.

How to transfer love to other pods: Kathleen Sebelius, a powerful politician, is the daughter of former Ohio governor J.J. Gilligan. She herself became the first female governor of Arkansas. She says that her mother took immense pride in her dad's political work, presenting it as impactful and akin to serving mankind. Hence, Kathleen was a part of her father's political journey, where she experienced at an early age how city councils were run, and how policies were discussed, formulated, presented and passed. She loved every bit of it because her dad cared deeply for his work, showed commitment to it and received much respect and recognition. Kathleen's husband, Gary Sebelius, came from a political family too, but his mother loathed politics. She disliked the long absences of her husband and never enjoyed the public service part of politics. When Kathleen married Gary, a magistrate judge, she openly communicated her choices and political ambitions.[81] Together, they created a shared context, but at the same time, respected the difference in their future choices. Her love for politics and public service did not dissuade her from partnering with someone who was not fond of her career choices. She rather let her love for the man and the job coexist.

Theatre veterans Shernaz Patel, Rajit Kapur and Rahul da Cunha have been partnering happily and successfully due to their common passion for theatre which led to the foundation of RAGE Productions, close to three decades ago. The popular English theatre company in Mumbai has given several original plays and adaptations to the audience which have been running for years. They call each other a 'three-sided see-saw' that is balanced on implicit trust and camaraderie.

Thus, the 'partner in you' helps the 'person', 'parent' and 'professional' in you become more connected through various ingredients of love. At the same time, it helps in transfer of learning to external partners.

3.   **Lessons from the 'Professional in You' to Other Ps:** Some unique experiences of a professional are worth emulating for other internal pods of a self-team. As mentioned in Chapter 2, the professional pod inherently has seeds of ambition, acumen and commitment which

---

[81]'Ep. 193 - Kathleen Sebelius from The Axe Files with David Axelrod', Stitcher, https://bit.ly/3CpUZuG. Accessed on 23 August 2022.

on acknowledgement, catalysis and preparation, enable an individual to excel. The wholesome definitions of these seeds are as follows:

a) **Ambition:** It is the desire for achievement, mostly personal. It lights up a constant fire for accomplishment of something that is considered valuable by the socio-cultural environment. Mostly, young children are shown academic brilliance as a token of accomplishment. Whatever is culturally accepted for a gender, race or age as an achievement, a person sets out to achieve. To infuse excellence in all walks of our lives, new narratives for ambition need to be written.

Let ambition cross the narrow by-lanes of personal grandeur and spread its wings into universal goodness. Our ambition today is to be intentional about where we put our attention to. Let your driving ambition be a holistic hero—a medley of many small giants rather than one big giant.

How to transfer ambition to other pods: Sarita Gupta and Ai-jen Poo migrated to the US from India and Taiwan, respectively. They carried their cultures of care with them. Poo grew up with her grandparents and parents. Her grandfather would practise tai chi in the driveway while her grandmother had an expansive view of family based on mutual care. In college, she volunteered for a domestic violence shelter, which inspired her to give voice to the unheard work of nannies, domestic helps and caregivers. Sarita faced the personal dilemma of attending to her young exuberant daughter and her frail parents who moved in with her. Together, they founded a national organization called Caring Across Generations, which aims to transform how we care for people, across the age spectrum.

Their ambition is no personal achievement, but to facilitate the 'Care Revolution'. Through her parent pod, Poo observed the lives of caregivers and domestic workers who worked relentlessly but were unable to take care of their own families. She has persuaded the world to take notice of the progression of the longevity of life. Many economists predict that care jobs including childcare and eldercare will form the largest single occupation in our workforce soon.[82] That is why Poo, as executive director of National Domestic Workers Alliance, is aiming at achieving well-being of all caregivers. She is partnering with government agencies to ensure that these women get enough pay, enough rest and enough respect. She sees the imbalance of power where these women work as, in her words, modern-day slaves. She works to bring more balance in their lives, which requires equal part tenderness and muscle. In most countries of the world, women work as caregivers, without any insurance or pay-offs. In the US, almost 47 per cent

---

[82]Manyika, James et al., *Jobs lost, jobs gained: What the future of work will mean for jobs, skills, and wages*, McKinsey & Company, 28 November 2017.

of caregivers are men, but they seem invisible and remain underpaid due to cultural conditioning.[83]

Poo and Gupta transfer ambition to all their pods by inspiring them to put undervalued work of nannies, domestic helps and caregivers at the pedestal of life. Their ambition meets at the intersection of gender and race and moves ahead to become more inclusive and meaningful for all. It moves forward to improve the life experience of oldsters as well as their caregivers by forming care grids and care squads. This is a wholesome ambition coming true, where Poo has won rights and protection for two lakh domestic workers in the state of New York, and 16,000 domestic workers in the state of Philadelphia got paid time off.

b) **Acumen:** On searching the word 'acumen' online, it doesn't show up on its own; it shows up as partnering with 'business' and stresses on 'business acumen'. This is one-dimension thinking. It comes from acuity; the ability of the mind to make good judgements and their application in life. We need acuity of mind to live a meaningful life, to make deep connections in relationships, to love our children, parents and pets, to make all of our life choices coherent and relevant. This acuity nudges us to make small changes in all spheres of our life to make big differences which compound over time. The use of acumen to specialize, and to earn money and prestige is a very narrow view of 'art of living'.

---

[83]MeetCareGivers, https://bit.ly/3lbB4FZ. Accessed on 16 May 2022.

Philosopher Roman Krznaric opines that a meaningful career should have five keys: earning money, achieving status, making a difference, following our passions and using our talents.[84] But he emphasized that they are not all created equal.

Though the desire to earn more money is widespread, our experience proves that money is a motivator till our important needs are met. After that, human beings look out for prestige. Here again, Krznaric advises that we should look for respect which we get owing to our individual contribution and not prestige related to social status. Let the professional pod profess acuity of mind.

How to transfer acumen to other pods: Professionals today look for more autonomy and less blind regimentation even when they work as employees. They use their acumen for 'job crafting'; they alter their identity at work by making their jobs more enriching, interesting and meaningful. A young teacher assistant at a business school was hired to assist senior faculty members in tutorials and administrative work. She made conversations with seniors to know them better and would share links of podcasts and online articles with them. She would refine their presentations by making them visually appealing and also teach students about self-management. She refused to be treated like a personal assistant ordering tea from the

---

[84]Popova, Maria, 'How to Find Fulfilling Work', The Marginalian, https://bit.ly/3GwWWWd. Accessed on 8 May 2022.

cafeteria for the seniors. Instead, she helped them with technology to create better pedagogical content.

The professional pod can help other internal pods learn 'role crafting'. A partner can learn to craft the daily tasks according to the need and interest. There are newly married couples whom I meet, where both love their ambitious jobs but dislike running errands and maintaining the home. They need to learn to craft their partnerial roles to include the good, the bad and the ugly for all. Both partners can tidy up their home every night, which allows them to sweep and vacuum thrice a week, wherein each might do it on Tuesday and Thursday and then do it together on Sunday. Parental pod should engage in 'cognitive crafting' to resolve conflicts with their growing children so that their relationships become more meaningful.

We need to sculpt our lives in such a way that we can minimize doing what irritates us and maximize doing what fulfils us. A mutual optimization of options is essential between the internal team of a person as well as the external teaming with siblings, spouse, founders or colleagues.

c) **Commitment:** Discipline smells of daily drudgery, something imposed, while commitment has a fragrance of deep connection with passion, from within.

Jack Gilbert was an American poet who received the Yale Younger Poets Prize for his first poetry collection, catapulting him into a celebrity poet and presenter. He immediately moved to Europe to escape the fame which he found boring and inconsequential. He published only five collections in a period of five decades but always continued writing poetry. He believed he was committed to poetry, not necessarily to publishing, giving readings, being reviewed or receiving prizes.

Let the professional pod develop a deep commitment to excellence in every chosen role. Let commitment be to the cause, not to the frills attached. When you sign up to become a soldier, you are committed to march. The same sentiment has been echoing amongst healthcare workers and doctors across countries after the deadly Covid-19 pandemic hit humankind. Many fought without protective gear, they faced the fear of their own looming deaths but stuck to their commitment to the community—to cure and if not cure, to heal.

How to transfer commitment to other pods: Professionals can transfer the learnings from commitment to other pods of personality easily. Brian Mullaney, a Harvard graduate, was 13 when he saw his younger sister, Maura, suffer and die from Stevens-Johnson Syndrome, which caused the top layer of her skin to peel off, turning her face and body into that of a 90-year-old. He fiercely resented the way everyone ostracized her based on her looks. He felt drawn to not let children be ridiculed due to deformities. The entrepreneur in him committed himself to start a charity called Smile Train, which helps in curing children with cleft lips. Unlike other charities, Mullaney runs it like a do-good brand for children's health. Rather than sending western doctors to perform cleft surgeries, Smile Train has developed state-of-the-art 3D technology to educate doctors in developing countries in these surgeries. The organization also conducts continuous field experiments to see what kind of donor incentives work best. It conducts one lakh surgeries a year. Mullaney has started WonderWork (wonderwork.org), which focusses on fixing five problems for poor children: blindness, club feet, burns, hydrocephalus and holes in the heart. Mullaney partners with doctors across the globe and empowers them with the know-how.[85] His professional pod is constantly reminded by his parent pod to persuade every doctor to make the lives of children better.

4. **Lessons from the 'Person in You' to other Ps:** The person pod, mostly the first pod, can teach the remaining pods to be authentic, creative and humble. We need to embrace the holistic definitions of these seeds for meaningful lives.

a) **Authenticity:** Each person pod has a seed of authenticity which enables them to be self-aware as well as socially aware. Authenticity nudges a person to find out what matters to him, which experiences

---

[85]Gneezy, Uri and John List, *The Why Axis: Hidden Motives and the Undiscovered Economics of Everyday Life*, Random House Business Books, 2015, pp. 208–209.

make him feel joyful, depressed, anxious, happy, disappointed or calm. Authenticity helps them to know deeply about what others feel or think. This seed helps them express themselves unapologetically and listen to others attentively. They love themselves but admit their own mistakes and love others too even if they are different. American research professor and lecturer Casandra Brené Brown says that authenticity means owning our story, embracing our vulnerabilities, knowing and celebrating our own imperfect selves.

This seed gives a person the courage to be who they are, not who they are expected to be.

How to transfer authenticity to other pods: The person pod should be mindful of subtle changes reverberating within. It should also be nudging each pod towards surprising themselves by staying open to unchartered territories.

Michelle Obama belonged to a stable, orderly African-American family in Chicago, where she and her brother were raised by their parents. Her elder brother got into Princeton University and she, too, was doing well in Whitney M. Young Magnet High School. When she went in for her first appointment with the school counsellor regarding her college admission applications, she announced her interest to join Princeton.

The counsellor patronizingly told her, 'I am not sure that you are Princeton material.'[86] However,

---

[86]Obama, Michelle, *Becoming*, Viking, 2018, pp. 65–66.

Michelle, rather than believing in the experienced judgement of the counsellor, believed in herself and gave it all, finally making it to Princeton. She never went back to the counsellor to tell her about getting accepted. After all, she was not doing it to show off or surprise her, but to 'be' herself, not someone she was expected to be.

Michelle continued to embrace herself as a professional, partner and a parent. She switched from her high-paying, highly perceived job as a lawyer to work at half the salary for the mayor of Chicago. She stayed true to the context of her life as she fell in love with a solitude-loving individualist and idealist like Barack Obama, while she herself was a fiercely ambitious and outgoing family person. As a parent, she surprised herself by becoming such an involved mother. Later, the political ambition of her partner gave her more opportune moments to stay true to her voice through the causes she endorsed and the active role she played as FLOTUS (First Lady of the United States). She wears her courage and vulnerability as a badge of honour through all the roles that she has chosen to play while preparing for her second innings as a thinker-author-change maker. Authenticity reverberates through all the domains of her life, making it look effortless and worthwhile.

b) **Creativity:** Creativity is identifying your talent and then working on honing it. Elizabeth Gilbert, one of the most creative souls of present times, says, 'The universe buries strange jewels deep within us all and then stands back to see if we can find them. The hunt to uncover those jewels—that's creative living.'

The seed of creativity gives courage to a person to find their hidden jewels. To be creative doesn't mean to be an artist, to be creative doesn't expect you to win some medals or rewards, it simply amplifies your life, making it more joyful and interesting—that is not easy, mind you. Every person has this seed of creativity which can be used like electricity, said Maya Angelou, to light up hallways or to electrocute. You can't use up creativity. The more you use it, the more you have it.

How to transfer creativity to other pods: The person pod can inspire all the pods to remain lifelong kindergarteners, ready to educate oneself consistently. As a kindergartener, a toddler is encouraged to imagine and develop his own ideas. Mitchel Resnick at MIT Media Lab has created four Ps of creative learning.[87] He believes that the best way to cultivate creativity is to support people working on projects based on their passion, in collaboration with peers and in a playful spirit. This is how a person pod can foster creativity for life, amidst all pods. A person catalysed with creativity can inspire the professional pod to use their curiosity to discover the hidden jewels of their ambition. They can guide the professional pod to take a road trip with creativity and fear. Since fear

---

[87]Resnick, Mitchel, 'Projects, passion, peers and play', https://bit.ly/3yFuKOW. Accessed on 16 May 2022.

never ceases to exist, a creative person can ask it to tag along in the back seat but without a voice and a vote. The person pod can suggest the partner pod to act creatively by marrying, multiple times, but the same person, over and over again, as Esther Perel states. Creativity can entitle the parent pod to create a listicle on 'Ten best ways to persuade teenagers' or 'Seven benefits of turning into a zero ego parent'.

c) **Humility:** It literally means having a 'low view of one's importance', but it shows us our right place. Being humble invites us to put others before us, to be thankful and sensitive. Humility installs compassion and gratitude—two qualities that are fast evaporating from the land of human heart. The person pod always has humility preprogrammed into it, what we need is to visit it and use it. From a very young age, it can show us to have an open mind, admit our mistakes, and to be considerate and vulnerable. It can also show us not to brag and be judgemental or stay hungry for attention. Humility makes us look at others, not for comparison but for compassion, for all.

How to transfer humility to all pods: 'Go out into a world where mankind is challenged, as it has never been challenged before, to prove its maturity and mastery—not of nature, but of itself,' wrote visionary marine biologist Rachel Carson in her path-breaking book *Silent Spring,* more than half a century ago.[88]

---

[88]Carson, Rachel, *Silent Spring,* Mariner Books; 40th Anniversary ed. Edition, 2022.

Though she did not live to see her work inspire the creation of Earth Day and the Environmental Protection Agency, she humbly kept working at showing us our real misdeeds and mishandling of nature and the environment.

All the other pods need to quickly be grateful to all that we get without spending a penny—the sunrise, the air, the rain, the water cycle, the ecosystem, the forests. Humility will make us sensitive before zooming out in our speeding car, splurging on accessories and mercilessly increasing our carbon footprints through world tours. The pandemic has given us a chance to listen to nature—the birds and the trees, the mountains and the seas. Let's change so that bioneers like Eve Ensler do not have to write an apology to Mother Earth—as species seem to be falling off the face of the earth, falling out of the dictionary, out of our consciousness, out of children's imagination. Let's self-inspect and humbly shoulder the personal responsibility and social accountability for the vanishing of birds, and forests being swallowed by our greed for concrete and human imprint on every piece of earth.

There is plenty of external transfer learning that happens when successful professionals like Satya Nadella and Daymond John inspire us to set excellent partnership goals, when a uniquely supportive parent like Leila Seth emboldens us to dance on the tightrope of professional and personal excellence. Respecting external transfer learning is a much-needed thought shift. Unless different pods of one's self-team meddle with different pods of my self-team to catalyse all of them, it would remain a one-dimensional life.

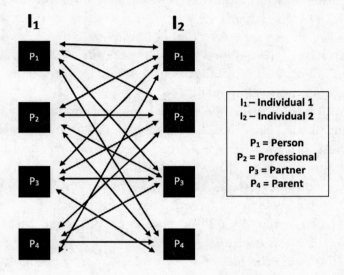

External Transfer Learning

For a holistic excellence-infused life experience, which is possible to achieve, all our pods should have something to offer, something to be proud of.

Beth Comstock, in her book *Imagining It Forward: Courage, Creativity, and the Power of Change,* shares how cockpit designers of an aircraft transfered their learnings to help create a solution for alarm fatigue experienced in an operation theatre (OT).[89] Alarm fatigue is a sensory overload that surgeons, anaesthetists and nurses experience when they

---

[89]Comstock, Beth and Tahl Raz, *Imagining It Forward: Courage, Creativity, and the Power of Change,* Virgin Digital, September 2018.

are exposed to an excessive number of alarms in an OT, which can result in desensitization to alarms and missed alarms. Patient deaths have been attributed to alarm fatigue.

The marketing team at General Electric (GE) was assigned with the task of finding a solution to this, for which they asked the question: who else faces such kind of a life-and-death situation while navigating through different inputs and monitory equipment?

They identified the cockpit as a place similar to an OT and invited pilots to observe surgeries. The pilots helped the GE team to create a three-screen machine similar to the three screens that aircrafts have.

Comstock used the same learnings personally for better time management. She created three segments in her mind: things I love to do, things I have to do and things I hate to do. Her aim became to maximize the first segment while outsourcing the second segment and minimizing the third one. This external transfer learning between people and philosophies, teams and trends increases the excellence quotient for each one.

TRADER JOE'S: A LEARNING HUB

They do not advertise but they are a chain of around 500 neighbourhood grocery stores. They do not offer any discounts, coupons or loyalty programmes, but they enjoy the grocery industry's highest sales per square feet. They discontinue many of their products ruthlessly when sales slow down or when prices soar, but thousands of people sign petitions to start a Trader Joe's in their vicinity.

The counterintuitive culture of this US-based chain makes it a loved brand which neither sells online nor delivers any product. The crew members believe that their store is their brand, what speaks for them.

If Trader Joe's can be considered an individual, it has its inner infrastructure well in place. It never brags about having the most exotic or extraordinary products, it has the products which are good enough for its customers. Trader Joe's means fun in buying food.

As a partner, it keeps customers first. If a customer asks for any help, the crew members are expected to drop everything they are doing to offer that help. There is very less hierarchy and everyone does everything. Each employee must have fun working at Trader Joe's or leave. All the employees work with agility and cohesion. Their biggest job is to talk to their customers, especially to have the letting-you-down conversation when their favourite product has been discontinued. The individual stores are decentralized to the extent that the captain (the store manager) runs the ship (the store). There is no corporate budgeting done at the centre. The captain sets the targets and prepares the budget for his store. Yet, the profits soar each year.

As a professional, it is committed to serve its customers and tutor them to believe in their product offerings. It has had only three CEOs in the last 60 years, which keeps it consistent. It is committed to offer a fun-filled, laid-back experience to its customers. They collect zero data from customers and somehow do not believe in adding new customers. They merely believe in retaining them. Their biggest marketing expense is food sampling in the absence of advertising of any kind. Customers are persuaded to sample their products at every store. Trader Joe's keeps itself equipped as a neighbourhood grocery store and doesn't intend to compete with stores like Whole Foods Market or Amazon that follow the standard methods. There is fluidity in its methods, where experience and wisdom matter more than analytics.

Every store is much smaller than any known grocery outlet as they do not give an overdose of options in products. They practise customer intimacy by giving priority to each customer. As a commercial enterprise, it offers much internal learnings to those who contribute to making Trader Joe's a loved brand. It offers a lot of learnings to the external world, too. Trader Joe's itself learns creativity and pivoting proactively from its P pods. It is a learning hub for each one of us who has begun to give up on all that which keeps us human— emotions, verbal communication, face-to-face interactions, fun, wisdom and excellence. Trader Joe's keeps its human side on. The promoters maintain silence and secrecy. Fun-loving foodies matter to them, fame doesn't. It encourages them to wear a Hawaiian shirt to work, to ring a bell to communicate to a colleague, to remember a customer by face (not their social media handles), to value each employee and to excel every day in every given task.

TRANSFER LEARNING NUGGETS

- There are different P pods in an individual that can be catalysed, simultaneously or sequentially. For excellence, each pod should sharpen the competencies it has.

- Then, each pod must transfer its learnings to other pods (internal transfer learning).
- Also, each pod must learn from and teach external resources mutual upskilling and enrichment (external transfer learning).
- The professional pod nurtures the innate seeds of ambition, acumen and commitment and then enables other pods to imbibe these qualities to become sharper at their jobs, with dedication.
- The parent pod nurtures the innate seeds of persuasion, egolessness and observation and then helps other pods become more persistent, attentive and egoless.
- The partner pod nurtures the innate seeds of shared context, power and love to make other pods more balanced, respecting and loving.
- The person pod nurtures the innate seeds of authenticity, creativity and humility and spreads these to all the other pods.
- Switch from one pod to another by pivoting with agility. Psych yourself up to attune yourself to enter the partner pod once you are out of office or to connect with the parent pod instantly if your child calls up at your workplace.
- Learn to navigate with agility between different roles.
- It helps to learn from a doctor if you are a pilot, it makes a lot of difference when a gender activist transfers their learnings to the parent in you. Such cross-pollination, such a fluid flow of experiences makes life wholesome.

PERENNIALLING

THE MAN WHO DIED AT 95 BUT LIVES ON

Born in Vienna, he was a rather lonely boy, not popular with his classmates. A house key and an alarm clock were symbolic of the onset of adulthood. He received them before he turned 14, but didn't use them. He loved the fact that a voice woke him up every day, not an alarm clock.

At 14, the school boy had a huge revelation. He was chosen as the youngest comrade flagbearer for a march organized by the Viennese young socialists' group on 11 November 1923 for freedom and equality under socialism. He was excited on getting this opportunity, more because it involved a tiny risk—he was short of turning 14 by eight days and no Viennese was allowed to participate in any political activity before turning 14. Though he marched with the flag for the longest time, he suddenly thrust the banner in the hands of a medical student standing behind him, left the march and headed home.

'I only found out that I don't belong,' he told his parents. This young boy grew up to be Peter Drucker, the thinker-author who is known as the father of management. When he was an eight-year-old, during the happenings of the First World War, Kranzgate became very popular as the first of the big 'war-profiteering' scandals. Meat was scarce and hence rationed. Sellers were supposed to sell it at a price fixed by the authorities.

Kranz, whose hotel was known for equality, bought decent meat from the black market, did not charge a penny more for meat dishes than what the law permitted, collected ration coupons and served portions of food as ration books permitted. What he intelligently did was to raise charges for unregulated items such as overnight stay at the hotel and the cover charge in the restaurant to compensate for the higher costs of the meat. He was suitably criticized socially and penalized. At a Christmas Party, eight-year-old Peter praised Kranz for trying to do the honourable thing. He gave his guests what they had come to expect, what he had promised them and what they were paying for, the young Peter reasoned. Peter not only became the only child who embarrassed his friends, but also a child who would always be admonished for speaking his mind. Peter Drucker left Vienna after high school and went to Germany, but left it when the Nazis came in.

As a teenager, friends of his parents, Hemme and Geniam, their full names being Dr Hermann Schwarzwald and his wife Dr Eugenie Schwarzwald, influenced him immensely through their choices and philosophies.

Hemme, the prodigal civil servant was a non-conformist, who made the unpopular career choices, steering clear of family support that could have got him the most plum jobs. Peter received some of his life's best advice from Hemme, whose words, abrasive but honest, persuaded him to leave Austria for London. Peter was lingering on his decision to leave and was prolonging his stay by making goodbye calls on everyone. During one of their meetings, Hemme said, 'Once one decides to leave, one leaves, one doesn't make farewell calls. Get up, go home and pack. The train for London leaves tomorrow noon and you are going to be on it.'[90]

Geniam, the enterprising woman, used to run a salon, a college preparatory school for women, a family camp and a co-op restaurant—as and when the need arose in her country, during pre-war, war and post-war. Peter observed that she was insensitive, which made her impervious to ridicule, criticism and embarrassment. What impressed Peter at that young age was her interest in achieving results for her goal—be it equality for women or getting nutritious food for families during war. The professional pod in him started getting shaped through these experiences.

In primary school, his principal-cum-homeroom teacher, Miss Elsa encouraged him and praised him for his reading, writing and arithmetic skills while nudging him to write two compositions in English every week. The art and craft teacher Ms Sophy gave young Peter a revolutionary doctrine to follow: boys should know how to sew and cook; girls should know how to sew and fix things—a great childhood

---

[90]Drucker, Peter F., *Adventures of a Bystander*, Routledge, 2017, p. 57.

lesson for Peter's self-team.

Peter Drucker, the doyen of management principles, believed that he learnt work discipline, goal setting and organizing from Miss Elsa and no one could have taught them better. Miss Elsa's work books, work plans and performance sheets saw him through his law school days too.

As a teenager, he realized the impact of the First World War on his country and on his life. Elders around him suffered from two emotions: pain and guilt. The pain of losing a complete generation of able leaders who lay in official cemeteries and the guilt of surviving with their deformed bodies, injured philosophies and broken dreams.

At 16, he left Vienna to become a trainee at an export firm in Hamburg. At the same time, a German economic quarterly published his article written on the Panama Canal's role in world trade which he had written as part of his university entrance exam. That was the beginning of the journey of an author of more than 60 books on sociopolitical synthesis and management.

He became a great intellectual partner of Fritz Kraemer, an American military educator and advisor, as they studied law at Frankfurt University and ran together the International Law seminar from 1929 to 1933. Their partnership, based on respect and trust, lasted a lifetime, despite differences in ideologies. Drucker observed that they asked similar questions though their approach to the answers was distinctly different. They would listen to each other as it helped both of them define themselves better. Despite ideological distinctiveness, Drucker helped Kraemer leave Germany and start afresh in the US. This developed his partnering abilities greatly.[91]

During this time, Peter worked as well as studied. Having started as a trainee in an export firm, he became a securities analyst in an old merchant bank before getting employment as a financial writer with Frankfurt's largest circulation newspaper. He earned a doctorate degree in international law, on the side. Drucker left Germany for England in 1933. In London, he worked for an insurance company, then as the chief economist at a private bank. There, he also reconnected with Doris Schmitz, whom he knew from his university days at Frankfurt. They married in 1934 and they then permanently relocated to the US, where he became a university professor, a writer and a business consultant.[92] In 1939, he wrote his first book, *The End of Economic Man: The Origins of Totalitarianism*. While he taught politics and philosophy at Bennington College from 1942 to 1949, he was invited to do a 'political audit' of General Motors (GM), one of the largest companies in the world then. On his GM experience was based his book *Concept of the Corporation*. This led to many other books and consultancy engagements. Drucker made management a liberal art and transferred learning from history, sociology, psychology, philosophy and culture to management. He not only wrote management books but also two novels and co-authored a book on Japanese paintings apart from writing columns and articles.

Drucker was a perennial who continued to move ahead in all his roles throughout his life. He progressed as a person

---

[91]Drucker, Peter F., *Adventures of a Bystander*, Routledge, 2017, p. 142.
[92]Ibid. 252.

by constantly educating and surprising himself. He partnered with various people, businesses and governments to refine his own ideas and thoughts while nurturing a family comprising his wife and four children. Drucker died in 2005. He was 95. His book *The Daily Drucker: 366 Days of Insight and Motivation for Getting the Right Things Done* was published in 2004 while three more books came out posthumously.

Not only this, his wife started a company at the age of 82 in 1993 and wrote her memoir *Invent Radium or I'll Pull Your Hair* in 2004 and lived up to the age of 103, thanks to her interest in exercise and competitive sports. She reinvented herself beautifully throughout her life, from being a lawyer and a physicist (in her thirties) and an entrepreneur (in her eighties) to a writer and speaker (in her nineties).

Peter and Doris Drucker lived a fulfilling life till the very end because they kept reinventing themselves. They maintained an active and disciplined lifestyle. Surprisingly, Doris played tennis and hiked till her mid-nineties. They always lived in more than one world, so to say, which is why they enjoyed diverse interests, activities, acquaintances and pursuits.[93]

On 11 April 2005, author Bruce Rosenstein interviewed Peter Drucker (all of 95) at the Claremont Graduate University campus, where he spoke about merging one's time and talent in a way that spreads across careers and relationships and promotes self-growth. He succeeded simultaneously in a portfolio of careers—writing, teaching

---

[93]Denning, Steve, 'How The Drucker Forum Was Born: A Tribute To Doris Drucker', *Forbes*, 3 October 2014, https://bit.ly/3OBay54. Accessed on 26 July 2022

and consulting—when everyone else was focussed on having just one career. He cultivated and nurtured partnerships, relationships, friendships across borders, organizations and governments. He excelled in maintaining professional and personal relationships since childhood and excelled in all P pods till the sunset of his life. He kept updating his previous books and presented a fresh and contemporary take in the revised editions, which made them even more successful. He mastered the art of staying relevant and sought after, deep into old age. He dabbled in a variety of careers which led him to meet different people from different walks of life—a very enriching experience indeed. He seamlessly transferred the learnings from the writer in him to the consultant in him to the partner in him. He effortlessly pivoted from writing about politics to writing about business and management to self-development. Catering to a wide range of readers, he stressed on planning for the second half of one's life. Yet, he didn't talk about excelling in different dimensions, i.e. as a partner (spouse) and a parent. He stressed on cultivating various interests like art or volunteering or reading. My philosophy of spicing up every aspect of our lives by embracing excellence 360 degree advocates perennialling in all the dimensions of our lives.

WHAT IS PERENNIALLING?

The lives of people like Peter Drucker, Ram Jethmalani, Mahashay Dharampal Gulati and Warren Buffett provide us with a wish and a way to be perennials. Drucker died at 95 living actively and excelling in various domains while

Jethmalani was active in Indian courts for more than 75 years. Even at the age of 96, Mahashayji, the owner of spices company MDH, was overseeing his business on a daily basis and Buffett, at 91, is still a force to reckon with in all investment matters.

Chandro Tomar from Johri village in India was a sharpshooting champion at the age of 87. Dame Judi Dench is a stellar film actor at 87, enjoying every minute in the spotlight. We need perennialling to become the rule. Perennialling means infusing the epilogue of our lives with excellence. It encourages us to lead a meaningful and beautiful post-retirement life.

Our lifestyle moving away from joint families to nuclear families to no families, from village to cities to a globalized world, from playgrounds to television to phone screens, from face-to-face non-stop chatter to phone talks to emojis, from festivals to greetings cards to WhatsApp forwards, from love to depression to loneliness, is a warning bell for our future selves. There are still some remnants of joint families and chunks of nuclear families around who watch TV, celebrate festivals, and maintain religious and spiritual faith but imagine the scenario after a quarter century. So many houses are getting permanently locked in our native places with the demise of parents while the young are being pushed to clear IITs or make it to the top world universities.

Despite secured pension and health insurance in developed nations, these people are battling a life-threatening problem—loneliness. In developing countries, loneliness compounded by financial problems will make life a long punishment. Mothers who are making children their only priority in life would be standing at a sad dead end after the children start their journey. In fact, former British prime minister Theresa May had appointed a 'Minister of Loneliness' to look into various problems and solutions around this new social epidemic that will engulf every country soon.[94]

We need to focus on all the Ps of our lives so that we have all the pieces working for us. Our professional piece needs to pivot into a way of work that earns purposeful busyness as well as some money for us. Our person piece needs to pivot into a space that we fill with unfinished dreams and long-forgotten hobbies. We need to create a happy space inside us.

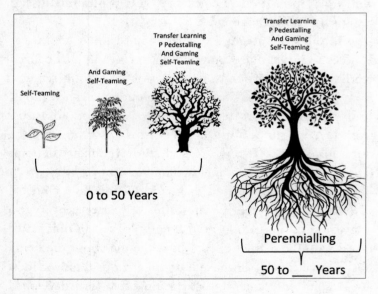

[94]John, Tara, 'How the World's First Loneliness Minister Will Tackle "the Sad Reality of Modern Life"', *Time*, 25 April 2018, https://bit.ly/3FlDQBs. Accessed on 6 May 2022.

You may start to SPYCE up at any juncture of your life. You may start to live a 5D life at any age. Give yourself a chance to live the various roles fully. Your internal team members will not change, your external team members might get replaced. When your children get busy with their lives, guide other children, mentor those who need support. When you retire, choose some work that adds purpose if not pennies. Teach a child, join a social group, volunteer at a non-profit organization. A person who only gets a high after meeting targets or by receiving social accolades will feel empty and lonely after a while. If he keeps all his Ps lubricated and well fed, his internal team will give him company.

In Japan, elderly women were deliberately shoplifting or indulging in petty crimes because they were finding it easier to live in prison than in domestic loneliness.[95] They were not prepared to tread on this long path of a lonely life. We need social engineering that would prepare the people to transition into senior citizenship with dignity.

HOW TO BE A PERENNIAL

a) Follow the Blue Zoners: Life is short. Don't run so fast that you miss it, said 107-year-old Raffaella Monne. This woman lives in one of the five 'Blue Zones', a term given to geographic regions that are home to some of the world's oldest people. The term was first used by the National Geographic author

---

[95]'Elderly people in Japan are getting arrested on purpose because they want to go to prison', *South China Morning Post*, 20 March 2018, https://bit.ly/38Rqr8d. Accessed on 6 May 2022.

Dan Buettner, who was doing a study on the places where people live exceptionally long lives.

During the course of their study, Buettner and his colleagues drew blue circles around these places on a map to distinguish them. That's how the term came into being. Buettner reiterates the belief that longevity is 20 per cent genetics and 80 per cent lifestyle choices.[96] These centenarians live in Okinawa, Japan; Sardinia, Italy; Nicoya, Costa Rica; Ikaria, Greece, and Loma Linda, California. Such centenarians are not found in great numbers in India. These Blue Zoners follow nine principles for a long life which is full of movement, happiness and purpose. These nine principles can enable us to stay agile, happy and relevant. Let's look at them:

i. *Move naturally:* Like Blue Zoners, we, too, should move our bodies physically throughout the day doing household work, gardening and walking.

ii. *Have a purpose:* Like these holistically healthy people, we, too, should have a purpose to get out of bed every day. Let us be on a daily mission to learn something new.

iii. *Down shift:* Like these golden agers, we, too, should de-stress like clockwork, creating our own stress-relieving rituals. Some pray, some play.

iv. *The 80 per cent rule:* Like these frugal eaters, we,

---

[96]Buettner, Dan, *The Blue Zones: Lessons for Living Longer from the People Who've Lived the Longest,* National Geographic; Reprint edition, 2010.

too, should stop eating when our stomachs are 80 per cent full, having our smallest meal in the early evening.

v. *Plant slant:* Like these right and light eaters, we, too, should consume more plants and vegetables, less carbs and meat.

vi. *Wine at 5:* Buettner's research shows that a moderate but regular consumption of wine with friends and food is a part of Blue Zoners' lifestyles. It will work only if other right principles are adhered to.

vii. *Belong:* Like these believers, we, too, must have faith in some spiritual or faith-inducing path.

viii. *Family first:* Like these family people, we, too, must believe in giving and receiving love which is a healthy practice achieved easily within a family.

ix. *Right tribe:* Like these longest-living people, we, too, must hang out with those friends and strong social networks that encourage us.

These habits need to be practised throughout life and all our roles should follow them without fail. No role should become an excuse for not being able to adhere to the Blue Zoner lifestyle.

b) Reinvent old-age expectations: Perennialling gives a new and fresh lease of life to those 'stay-at-home' moms and dads who missed the professional bus in their younger years owing to family responsibilities.

The idea that careers traditionally get built before the age of 40 is outdated now. Some talent might start blooming in the forties and blossom in the sixties and seventies. Age as an aspect of careers is losing its importance because linear trajectories of unidimensional job experience are not enough now.

'The fifties was the most exciting career decade of my life so far. And it looks like my options are only getting better as I turn 60,' says Babette Pettersen, who was head hunted by a sustainable chemicals company BioAmber as VP Chief Commercial Officer when she was in her fifties and then she shifted to a start-up.

Revathi Roy, a serial entrepreneur in India, started her first venture, Asia's first women cab service, at the age of 47. In the last 14 years, she has launched the women-only last-mile parcel delivery service, and won many awards and accolades while empowering thousands of urban poor women. She looks forward to a meaningful career ahead.

India's finance minister Nirmala Sitharaman, 62, debuted in Indian politics nearly 14 years ago, joining the Bhartiya Janata Party and starting a new career.

Judy Dench's and Robert De Niro's achievements, at their age, should alter the way we think about career phases, career development and retirement. Life is fluid and so should be careers, especially for women. Why should the body clock and career clock be chiming together, forcing women to give up one for the other? Careers can flow fluidly till late if the bodies cannot wait. Women rediscovering themselves after leading successful parenthood years should be the norm.

In a study titled 'How Age and Gender Affect Self-Improvement', Jack Zenger and Joseph Folkman found that older people were more open to self-improvement and less defensive to self-criticism.[97] This was truer for women who have an accelerated evolving self, well into their sixties, when men start to decline. Women are better at weathering the storm of youthful cronyism—the tendency of the young to hire the young, as they are more adaptable to blend in without ego. Women are walking out of their marriages, even late in their lives, if they are not given the freedom to exercise their choice. 'Silver' or 'grey' divorces are on a rise.[98]

In 2014, people aged 50 and above were twice as likely to go through a divorce as in 1990, according to the National Centre for Family and Marriage Research at Bowling Green State University, Ohio, US.[99]

This is so because life expectancy is on the rise. Divorce is not as stigmatized as it used to be. Most of the grey divorces (60 per cent) are initiated by women as they become more empowered, decisive and free from responsibilities as a parent.

---

[97]Zenger, Jack and Joseph Folkman, 'How Age and Gender Affect Self-Improvement', *Harvard Business Review*, 5 January 2016, https://bit.ly/3yzwNEf. Accessed on 5 May 2022.

[98]Ellin, Abby, 'After Full Lives Together, More Older Couples Are Divorcing', *The New York Times*, 30 October 2015, https://nyti.ms/3pEeXtW. Accessed on 23 August 2022.

[99]Ibid.

According to UN Population Statistics database, India will add another 183 million people to the working age group of 15–64 years between 2020–50. There is enough scope for the growth rate of women labour force at 20 per cent to grow further.[100] All those qualified others who joined the workforce at the turn of the century in various traditional and non-traditional job opportunities but took a break for personal reasons would be ready to make a comeback. These women, backed by life experiences, matured by reflecting on world events, and upgraded by knowledge and courses in chosen fields, would be a rich source for decision-making, creative thinking, negotiating, conflict resolving and mentoring roles.

Retaining women, at home and at work, requires self-awareness and a new mindset. The realities of today need a recalibration of expectations from both men and women. At work, it means welcoming talent late in one's career, without having ageist blinders on. At home, it needs a strategic focus on enhancing the potential of both partners, attentive listening and need fulfillment. To retire or to re-fire, that is the question.

Roopa Kudva, former CEO of CRISIL, heads Omidyar Networks, an impact investing firm. She says that there is a lot of talk and discussion around women dropping out of their professions when they

---

[100]Can India's demographic dividend turn into liability? Read here', Livemint, 3 April 2022, https://bit.ly/3zycwPi. Accessed on 26 July 2022.

start a family.[101] But there is less recognition of the second road block that women generally hit when they reach the tail end of middle management or enter senior management. Women hold back and do not ask for the top jobs and hence, do not get them as often as they should. She feels surprised that everyone talks about 'preparing women for board roles or senior roles' when no one talks about 'preparing men for the same roles'.

Self-preservation is as important as generosity. Perennialling suggests women to present themselves for the senior roles as the most natural progression of their careers.

c) Introduce 'late life advisors' as a career option: We are turning into a consumerist society, where the youthful and saleable are glorified while the old and cherishable are marginalized. As we become more individualized, we care less for the family, especially the elderly. As we become more globalized, we leave behind our native places, our parents and embrace the shiny city life. As we become more technology enslaved, we get obsessed with a virtual world and the real world with real problems becomes a burden. We are unprepared to manage our old age with full vigour and happiness. With lowering mortality rates, we will be living longer than ever and we need to prepare to live it up in a wholesome

---

[101]'316: 29.03 Roopa Kudva–Growing through the ranks at CRISIL', Podcast9, https://bit.ly/3FRFjQA. Accessed on 16 May 2022.

way. Old age is not a handicap; it is a truth that needs to be invested in with thoughtful decisions in our youth. Staying healthy and physically active, mentally agile and psychologically nourished has to be a long-term goal during the busy years of our life when we are preoccupied with professional work and family commitments. A healthy body with an agile mind is the self-insurance we need to save ourselves from the social prejudice called 'ageism'. Marginalizing the elderly is a mistake we have been socially committing for years.

'With whom, where and how will I want to spend my time after I turn 70?' is a very valid question we need to ask ourself by the time we turn 60. Though the seeds of this plan should be planted by the time we hit 50, we need to plan and prepare for meaningful later decades. Just like we have a financial advisor, an education advisor at universities, we must have an old age advisor who plans to invest their time with us after we turn 60. We need to launch a new educational degree in old-age management which would create a complete set of professionals enabling older people to live a more productive and wholesome life. As the geriatric population increases in number, the younger and the older people would need to co-create an ecosystem where 'ageing well' is prioritized and considered a life goal.

We need late life advisors as emotional enablers because families are breaking much faster, leaving people to build their lives on their own. We need late life advisors as physical supporters who can assist in managing daily chores and daily nostalgia. We need late life advisors to prepare us mentally to think about a 'Future Me', who would fit into the accelerating world with ease.

The biggest problem of humanity is going to be irrelevance, not exploitation, says thinker Yuval Noah Harari. Though most of the sectors and industries will be conquered by AI by 2050, the human care industry will remain a human bastion for a long time.[102] Hence, late life advisors would be a viable and safe career option for a long time.

d) Break geriatric stereotypes: Midlife and later-life need to be seen with fresh eyes and lived with a fluid mindset where age should not be the hero. Excellence 360 degree advocates a knock out of three types of geriatric stereotypes: personal, professional and social.

Personal stereotypes: If you compare a photograph of your parents and your grandparents when both were in their sixties, you will notice that your parents looked much younger at that age. Chances are you, too, will look much younger than your parents when you are in your sixties. As we live longer lives, our cultural conditioning around age needs to change. Associating tiredness and the feeling of having done enough with age is passé. Our self-team needs

---

[102]Hern, Alex, 'Technology in 2050: will it save humanity—or destroy us?' *The Guardian*, 3 January 2020, https://bit.ly/3shPet0. Accessed on 6 May 2022.

to embrace age agnosticism. There are people who structure their lives around age, but there is an increasing tribe who centre their lives by not centring it anywhere for long.

Some choose to study-marry-work, others chose to work-marry-study. People delay work to raise children. People delay children to work. Similarly, we should make ourselves ready to keep the second half wholesome with better focus on health and medical facilities, the feeling of feeling old needs a course correction. Our self-team needs to infuse 'feeling fit' till the end of the tunnel from the beginning.

Each one of us needs to stay curious and master the art of asking questions, not answering. A person who readily asks questions without feeling shy or conscious will seamlessly run into unchartered waters and unplanned discussions. Our self-team needs the courage to ask questions—the basic ones, the silly ones, more than once, even when there are no answers. Asking questions prepare us as a seeker, as opposed to standing on a cliff not knowing what lies ahead. This feeling propels us to become a perennial for life.

Khushwant Singh, a prominent novelist, historian, journalist, columnist, editor, a grandfather, father and husband, stayed active till 99.

In today's time, even rigidity cannot stay rigid. We need to give away our behavioural 'bricks' to turn them around into behavioural brooks. Our self-team needs to free itself from our past failures as well as successes. It will help in decluttering our heads and hearts. Our self-team needs to learn to sit feather light on past laurels. Grandparents cannot deal with their grandchildren while keeping in mind how they raised their own children. A successful CEO in the last decade needs to get out of the old and snug costume of success to get into the new dress of a learner.

American hotelier and hospitality entrepreneur Chip Conley refers to it as the readiness to move from 'sage on the stage' to 'guide on the side', something he did personally when Brian Chesky, Airbnb co-founder, invited him to join his company as mentor, leaving behind his CEO status at Joie de Vivre, his own hotel group.[103] Starting on a clean slate every few years with curiosity and sans ageism will help in becoming a perennial.

Professional stereotypes: In their later years, professionals need to play on their wisdom culled out from knowledge accumulated over the years. To attain knowledge, we add things every day, while to attain wisdom, we remove things every day. Midlife professionals should leave their boss baggage behind to begin a liberated journey which is unscripted. In the movie, *The Intern*, Ben Whittaker (Robert De Niro), starred as a 70-year-old intern in Jules Ostin's (Anne Hathaway) fast-growing e-commerce fashion start-up. After a few weeks at the organization, he becomes a 'mentern' (mentor plus intern), who mentors privately and interns publicly. Baked seniors can mentor microwaved millennials in listening, patience and deep learning, while quick millennials can encourage slow seniors to communicate concisely and respond in real time. The Ewing Marion Kauffman Foundation reports that professionals between 50 and 65 years of age are 65

---

[103]Conley, Chip, *Wisdom at Work: The Making of a Modern Elder*, Portfolio Penguin, 2019, p. 35.

per cent more likely to found a new company than those between 20 and 34.[104] Older people are breaking stereotypes by thinking about retiring from one job as re-firing for the next career. They are ready to learn the shared language of respect and collaboration while creating a portfolio of sequential as well as simultaneous careers. They understand the need for consistent upgradation and pivoting.

Falguni Nayar went from being the stellar managing director of Kotak Mahindra Capital Company, to being a sought-after e-commerce entrepreneur, riding on a ₹5,000-crore business Nykaa, in less than a decade. A holistic hero, Falguni has excelled in all her roles as a person, partner, parent and professional with a pivot that has brought her twin children into the business fold with her.

Professionals must consider midlifers and late-lifers as a big target segment of consumers, not only for products like hearing aids, diapers or hospitals but for other innovative products too. For example: Saregama India Ltd created a simple radio-like gadget called 'Carvaan', which enabled music lovers to choose from a collection of 5,000 handpicked high-quality songs by legends like Lata Mangeshkar, Kishore Kumar, Manna Dey, Mukesh, Asha Bhosle and Jagjit Singh, to name a few. The songs are classified into artists, moods and Ameen Sayani's priceless collection of Geetmala. This innovative idea won Saregama the 'Innovation of the Year' award at the Brand Equity Marketing Awards 2018.

The product is sturdy, simple, without apps and with big buttons. Navin Talreja, the founder of The Womb,

---

[104]Ozkal, Derek, 'Millennials can't keep up with boomer entrepreneurs', Kewing Marion Kauffman Foundation,19 July 2016.

the advertising agency that worked on Carvaan, says, 'In a market where everyone wants to target the young and create meaningless apps and tech, comes a meaningful innovation fulfilling a specific need of a target segment nobody creates anything for: the 50+. It is something people have special emotional relationship with.'[105]

The professional stereotype of 'I want to be the most knowledgeable and hence most authoritative in the room' is diluting. If you are smartest in the room now, you are in the wrong room, is the fluid credo of future. Wear your wisdom, not knowledge on your sleeve. Flaunt a fluid mindset, not a fixed or a growth mindset. Plan for midlife career and late-life career, not retirement. Expand your portfolio of pursuits.

Social stereotypes: 'With age comes diseases' is a stereotype that needs to be shattered. Age does not necessarily entail the onset of diseases, and we have the Blue Zoners to prove that. Getting old is getting bold—with choices and challenges cushioned by wisdom collected over years. Rather than discriminating dotage, we need to dignify it. Late lifers are not obsolete people who should give up their autonomy because it is expected of them. A senior surgeon-journalist-author-son-father-husband, Atul Gawande, synonymous with following the pillars of excellence 360 degree, writes: 'Safety is what we want for those we love and autonomy is what we want for ourselves.' In the name of safety, youngsters intend to stifle the autonomy of elders which they do not like, which is why most of the elders decide to stay alone.

---

[105]Bhatt, Shephali, 'Carvaan: A product NOT targeted at Gen Y or Gen Z', *The Economic Times*, 7 October 2017.

The social stereotype of making seniors live longer anyhow, should be shunned.

Dignified dotage requires a two-pronged strategy. First, be a part of your parent's journey moving forward in the eighth and ninth decade of their lives. Rather than restricting and controlling their lives, let them cherish the joy of doing things, no matter how small, independently. It will go a long way in boosting their confidence. Observe and feel the changes that they have gone through and empathize with their present.

In his book, *Being Mortal: Medicine and What Matters in the End*, Gawande talks about a Stanford experiment where incidents of depression and overall ill health reduced when a nursing home opened its door to four cats, two dogs, 100 birds and children. It humanized the atmosphere and made the patients lively.[106] Second, your experience with your parents will help you plan for your geriatric journey better and in time. So, let us dignify our dotage by observing our parents and then planning for our own.

A social acceptance of age agnosticism is on the cards where chronological age is merely a number for reference. Why should colleges be filled with 20-somethings only? Why can't people in their fifties pursue a gap year? Why do we feel surprised to see a smiling 70-year-old behind a hotel reception desk, ready to check us in? These are the questions that Chip Conley asks in his book *Wisdom at Work*.[107]

Age agnosticism will nudge us towards accepting people

---

[106]Gawande, Atul, *Being Mortal: Medicine and What Matters in the End,* Metropolitan Books; 1st edition, 2014.
[107]Conley, Chip, *Wisdom at Work: The Making of a Modern Elder*, Portfolio Penguin, 2018, pp. 47.

in action anywhere, anytime, age notwithstanding. Elizabeth White, at 55, has started Resilience Circles to bring people like her together, to give them the confidence that they are evolving while staying authentic.

Generation gap should transform into intergenerational transfer of trust, respect and learning. A fluid mindset that flows between different roles, different careers and different generations will be the hallmark of an excellence-infused life. Three generations in a meeting or on a dining table, making merry and taking decisions can be a reality. Unless a collaborative transfer of knowledge and constant upgradation of skills is achieved among people born a decade apart, no future job being safe from automation, a large section of society will become redundant. Our society will not only be struggling with better-skilled humans or humans upgrading themselves using machines but also against self-learning machines. It is no big news that a computer defeated a human at chess. Google's AlphaZero program learnt chess in four hours through self-learning and defeated Stockfish 8, the world's computer chess champion in 2016. There is no survival without fluidity and flexibility in any role. Keep priorities of life fluid.

Stay in tune with your bodies. During the prehistoric age, human beings used their mindfulness to pay attention to their surroundings. They kept a close tab on whatever they smelled, touched, saw, tasted and heard. They could predict a tsunami in advance. They could differentiate between poisonous and edible mushrooms. They relied on alertness and attention to save themselves from animal or tribal attacks, unlike today, when our attention is fixated on our smartphones, while we collect food from aisles of malls and eat them hastily, glued to our screens. Historian and author Noah Harari says, 'Humans have bodies. During the last century, technology has been distancing us from our bodies... People estranged from their bodies, senses and physical environment are likely to feel alienated and disoriented.'[108]

Since our perception of ourselves is largely dependent on how others see us, courtesy likes on our social media profiles, we are getting disconnected from our own selves. Harari aptly warns us that if we don't feel at home in our bodies, we will never feel at home in the world.

Rather than connecting with thousands of people online, let us reconnect with our bodies for perennial—mental, emotional, spiritual and physical—well-being.

JUSTICE LEILA SETH: EXCELLING TILL THE END

The first woman chief justice of a State High Court in India, a mother of three, a loving and supportive wife, a barrier breaker all her life, Leila Seth, ran the marathon of life with all the P pods hopping side-by-side.

Born and raised in a gender-equal family, she studied at Loreto Convent in Darjeeling and then took up the job of a stenographer in Kolkata. She met Prem Nath Seth and soon they were married. Prem moved to London with Leila and their little baby where Leila used the opportunity to study further, took the London Bar exam and became

---

[108]Harari, Yuval Noah, *21 Lessons for the 21st Century,* Random House; 1st Edition, 2018, pp. 88–89.

the first women to top it in 1958. They soon returned to India and she cleared the Indian Civil Services exam too. Simultaneously running her partnerial and parental journeys, she joined the Patna High Court as a junior. She practised for a few years despite getting less work because gender came first and merit second. She had two more children but continued to work for a senior lawyer. After 10 years, in 1972, she moved to the Delhi High Court. She took up varied matters: criminal matters, taxation matters, writ petitions, revisions and appeals.

When she was appointed as the first female judge of the Delhi High Court, she was treated as an outsider. Her Delhi Gymkhana Club membership was rejected as it was meant only for male judges.

While raising her two boys and a daughter, she persisted and was appointed as the Chief Justice of Himachal Pradesh High Court in 1991.

Recounting her experience, she said, 'In most cases, male lawyers or judges especially in upper Himachal had a feudal mentality. They were not used to a woman sitting on their head. But as I was a mother of two boys, I knew how to handle men sensitively. I would gently ask their opinions first before imposing mine on them.'[109]

She was a part of 15th Law Commission of India that transformed inheritance laws for women as well as the Justice Verma Committee instituted after the Nirbhaya gangrape.

Though people judged the choices she made, she never

---

[109]Manglik, Tanya, 'The Lady of Law and Love: A Tribute to Justice Leila Seth', Feminism in India, 18 July 2017, https://bit.ly/3yFtBqp. Accessed on 16 May 2022.

shied away from living her life fully, as a spouse and as a mother. She always stood by the choices her children made, even when her son, Vikram Seth, came out as gay. She used her life experiences and sensitivity to write books for children, to support minority rights and to promote gender equality. She remained agile and active till her death in 2017. She is an inspiration not just for the legal community but for all.

PERENNIALLING NUGGETS

- Start to plan about infusing the epilogue of your life with excellence as soon as you hit 50 (40 ain't bad either).
- Focus on all the Ps of your life so that they are working in sync by the time you near retirement.
- When you retire, choose some work that adds a pep and purpose, if not pennies.
- Follow the nine principles of the Blue Zoner lifestyle.
- Embrace age agnosticism.
- Believe that body clocks of women can't wait but career clocks can.
- Grey divorces are rising across the globe, so redefining marriage is a must.
- Campaign for 'late-life advisors' as a career option to co-create an ecosystem for ageing well.
- Knock out three types of geriatric stereotypes: personal, professional and social.
- Some study-marry-work. Some work-marry-study. Some delay work to raise children. Some delay children. It's all fluid till the end.

- Turn behavioural bricks into behavioural brooks. Be ready to turn from 'sage on the stage' to 'guide on the side'.
- If you are the smartest person in the room, you are probably in the wrong room. Drop that ego and run to be a mentern—mentor in private and an intern in public.
- Age and disease are not congruent. Don't discriminate against dotage, dignify it.
- In the name of safety, youngsters should not snatch the autonomy from their elders.
- Observe your parents, humanize the atmosphere for them and plan your own dotage.

EPILOGUE

Are you ready?

If you are on this page, I safely assume that you are an excellence 360 degree enthusiast, ready to excel at anything and everything.

It is certainly not an easy way out when you choose to be a holistic hero, but it is worth it.

Be a 'self teamer'. You will never be lonely. Your P pods will form your trusted team for keeps. Nourish all of them. They will not disappoint you. You will have soulmates in solitude for life.

Be an 'and gamer'. We are already centuries behind our schedule. For how long can we play the lopsided game of patriarchy which does not even offer a level playing field to all players? Level the field and join hands. Make bed and make money—together. While she files a tax return, finish the laundry. And don't exert to be a supermom. He can do many things and better. Let your son cry. Let your daughter kick. Or whatever.

Be a 'P Pedestaller'. Let all the P pods stand together

on a plank-like pedestal. Work and life are fluid. Integrate both, create harmony. Value your parent perspective before launching a product. Value your professional perspective before strategizing how to talk to your teenager.

Work from home. Work at home. Feel at home at work.

Be a 'transfer learner'. What are you hoarding your knowledge for? Cross-pollination makes the yield better for all. Prep yourself up for getting in and out of your P pods nimbly and simply, many times a day. Pat yourself for your agility and patience.

Be a 'perennial'. Expect to age. Welcome those wrinkles. Ageing is living. Planning to retire? Reignite your talents instead. Give equal parts autonomy and safety to your parents. Dignify dotage, for them and for yourself. Think about your next career. Today.

Hope to see you somewhere on this eternal journey to excellence, with all your P pods.

ACKNOWLEDGEMENTS

A big thank you to:

- All the parents and children who came to Swash, and put their trust and faith in me.
- All the colleagues at different workplaces, who, directly or indirectly, pushed me to ask tougher and new questions.
- All the members of my mental community, the people I spend most of my time with: podcasters, authors, thinkers, change makers. Though I have not met all of you in person, you form my world.
- My four parents and my daughter, for enabling me to play my roles. Thank you for the tough love.
- My husband, for being the centre of the many waves I surfed.
- Rudra Narayan Sharma at Rupa Publications, for all the long chats and detailed discussions.
- Manali Das from Rupa Publications for a detailed copy-edit.
- Mamta and Dharmendra, for constantly assisting their technologically challenged seniors.
- Last but not least, all the readers who visit my blog and help me fight my biggest demon: self-doubt.